You Could Drive a Person Crazy
---◆---

You Could Drive a Person Crazy

♦

Chronicle of an American Theatre Company

Scott Miller

New Line Theatre

Writers Club Press
New York Lincoln Shanghai

You Could Drive a Person Crazy
Chronicle of an American Theatre Company

All Rights Reserved © 2002 by Scott Edward Miller

No part of this book may be reproduced or transmitted in any form or by any means, graphic, electronic, or mechanical, including photocopying, recording, taping, or by any information storage retrieval system, without the written permission of the publisher.

Writers Club Press
an imprint of iUniverse, Inc.

For information address:
iUniverse
2021 Pine Lake Road, Suite 100
Lincoln, NE 68512
www.iuniverse.com

ISBN: 0-595-26311-9

Printed in the United States of America

"Congratulations to New Line Theatre,
and thanks from everybody who cares about musicals
for its continued support and exploration."

Stephen Sondheim
November 22, 2000

Contents

New Line Theatre's First Ten Seasons At a Glance 1
The Story of New Line 3
Remembering the First Ten Years 20
A Tribute to the Rock Musicals 2 30
Attempting the Absurd 37
Smokin' Santa 41
A Tribute to the Musicals of Stephen Sondheim 43
A Tribute to the Dark Side 2 48
Breaking Out in Harmony 53
Assassins 57
Pippin 64
In the Blood 70
Company 74
Out on Broadway 78
Sweeney Todd 84
Passion 89

Jacques Brel is Alive and Well and Living in Paris *95*
The Ballad of Little Mikey *100*
Extreme Sondheim *104*
March of the Falsettos *109*
Woman With Pocketbook *112*
Assassins *116*
Party *123*
Songs for a New World *128*
Camelot *135*
Into the Woods *144*
Head Games *151*
A New Line Songbook *156*
Floyd Collins *157*
Out on Broadway 2000 ...... *167*
Hair *171*
A New Line Cabaret *182*
Cabaret *183*
Anyone Can Whistle *191*
Hair *199*
Move On *209*
New Line's Biggest and Most Loyal Supporters During the First Ten Years *212*
About the Editor *217*

New Line Theatre's First Ten Seasons At a Glance

◆

1991-1992
A Tribute to the Rock Musicals 2
Attempting the Absurd

1992-1993
Smokin' Santa
A Tribute to Stephen Sondheim

1993-1994
A Tribute to the Dark Side 2
Breaking Out in Harmony
Assassins

1994-1995
Pippin
In the Blood

1995-1996
Company
Out on Broadway
Sweeney Todd
Out on Broadway

1996-1997
Passion
Jacques Brel
The Ballad of Little Mikey

1997-1998
Extreme Sondheim
March of the Falsettos
Woman with Pocketbook
Assassins

1998-1999
Songs for a New World
Camelot
Into the Woods

<u>1999-2000</u>
A New Line Songbook
Floyd Collins
Out on Broadway 2000
Hair

<u>2000-2001</u>
A New Line Cabaret
Cabaret
Anyone Can Whistle
Hair

<u>Out of Line Productions</u>
Party, August. 1998
Head Games, August 1999

The Story of New Line

It was 1991 and Scott Miller was running a community theatre group named CenterStage Theatre Company with his high school drama teacher Judy Rethwisch. He had also been working for Dance St. Louis for four years, learning arts administration under the tutelage of veteran arts administrator Adam Pinsker. After seven years of community theatre, producing and directing good but safe musical theatre, Miller was getting restless. He wanted to take some risks. Emboldened by all he was learning from Pinsker, Miller left CenterStage to form a new theatre company.

The new company was called New Line Theatre (no, there was no particular reason for the name; it just sounded good), and from the beginning it was something different. New Line was envisioned as an alternative musical theatre company, producing issue-oriented musicals and revues, including world premieres, St. Louis premieres, and important Broadway and off-Broadway shows.

During New Line's first ten seasons, friends teased Miller that New Line would only produce a musical if someone in it died at the end. It was a joke, but not all that far from the truth. Though all New Line's shows don't fall into that category, quite a few do—*Assassins, In the Blood, Sweeney Todd, Passion, Jacques Brel, The Ballad of Little Mikey, Woman with Pocketbook, Songs for a New World, Into the Woods, Floyd Collins,* and *Hair*—more than a third of the shows New Line has produced. And in addition to those, leading characters almost die in *Pippin* and *Camelot*, and some of them are about to die in *Cabaret*.

New Line's first few seasons were anchored by "tribute" concerts, an invention Miller brought with him from CenterStage. Each of these tributes focused on one songwriter, one genre, or one subject. New Line's first show was *A Tribute to the Rock Musicals 2* (the first *Tribute to the Rock Musicals* had been produced by CenterStage), at the Center of Contemporary Arts. This evening of songs from rock and pop musicals included numbers from *Hair, Godspell, Jesus Christ Superstar, Grease, Pippin, The Wiz, The Rocky Horror Show, Working, Evita, Dreamgirls, Joseph and the Amazing Technicolor Dreamcoat, Little Shop of Horrors, Cats, Chess, Miss Saigon,* and other shows. *A Tribute to the Rock Musicals 2* took audiences on a walking tour of the development of rock and pop music on and off Broadway. Bob Wilcox of *The Riverfront Times* praised "the impressively—sometimes overwhelmingly—enthusiastic, talented, skilled, and well-trained cast and band."

The second show New Line produced was a new musical with book, music, and lyrics by Scott Miller. It was called *Attempting the Absurd*, a post-modern, self-referential musical farce that told the story of a young man who has figured out he's only a character in a musical comedy and doesn't really exist. Naturally everyone around him thinks he's nuts, but he proves them all wrong at the end of the show by pulling out the script for *Attempting the Absurd*. Harry Weber of *The Riverfront Times* called the show "about as good an evening of first-view musical comedy as I've seen for a while."

New Line's second season opened with a revue and celebrity auction at the Center of Contemporary Arts. The auction included autographed items from Julie Andrews, Jerry Herman, Bob Hope, Hal Prince, Gwen Verdon, Elaine Strich, Raul Julia, Jim Lapine, Harnick and Bock, Kander and Ebb, Schmidt and Jones, William Daniels, Paul Gemignani, Marvin Hamlisch, Jean Stapleton, Patricia Zipprodt, Michael Feinstein, and many other Broadway stars.

In December, the season continued with an off-beat revue of Christmas songs called *Smokin' Santa,* and then another tribute, this time one to Stephen Sondheim. *Smokin' Santa* contained a few original songs, such as "The Christmas Tree Fell Over and Our House is Burning Down," several parody numbers, like Dan Guller's "The Song About Hanukkah" (to the tune of "America" from *West Side Story*), some pseudo-standards like "You're a Mean One, Mister Grinch," some traditional carols, and even a couple classical pieces. The *Tribute to Stephen Sondheim* was a tour of the musical theatre career of the legendary Broadway composer Stephen Sondheim, stretching from *West Side Story* in 1957, up to *Assassins* in 1991, showcasing both Sondheim's popular songs and his more obscure pieces. Stephen Sondheim became an honorary board member in 1993, making this concert even more special for the company.

The 1993-94 season opened with a third tribute, this time *A Tribute to the Dark Side 2*, the title soon shortened to just *Dark Side 2* (again, the first *Tribute to the Dark Side* had been a CenterStage show). A fascinating evening of theatre songs about murder, lust, adultery, greed, betrayal, despair, and deceit, the production included songs from *Little Shop of Horrors, Grand Hotel, City of Angels, Guys and Dolls, Grease, Sweet Charity, Mack and Mabel, Chicago, Working, Show Boat, Dreamgirls, Company, Jesus Christ Superstar, Promises Promises, Les Misérables, Miss Saigon,* and other shows. For this production, the company moved to the New City School Theatre, where the rent was cheaper and where they'd be closer to St. Louis' Central West End, one of the city's cultural hot spots.

The season continued with another original book musical from Scott Miller, *Breaking Out in Harmony,* based on the true story of a book banning case in a high school. A few audience members were offended enough by the show's politics that they walked out during performances. The show received mixed reviews, but Harry Weber said in *The Riverfront Times* that "Some of *Breaking Out*'s songs are rousers." Joe Pollack wrote in the *St. Louis Post-Dispatch,* "There are a lot of truths—

and a lot of questions in *Breaking Out in Harmony*…the questions must be asked and answered, even though they often are very painful…In many respects, [author Scott Miller] has dealt with it well. He is fair to both the parents and the students, allowing both sides to make a case even though it's pretty obvious where his sympathy lies…Despite the shortcomings, Miller has written a show that is 'about something,' and about something important too…It's worth seeing, thinking about, and most important, acting on." But the New Liners knew they had hit a real hot-button topic when one local woman was enraged enough by the politics of the piece that she wrote a letter to the editor of *The Riverfront Times* about the show. Thus began New Liner's serious love affair with issue-oriented musicals.

Though New Line thought the company would be saving money at New City School, it turned out the space was not very well equipped and expenses were almost as high as they had been at the Center of Contemporary Arts. So New Line moved again, this time to the St. Marcus Theatre, a small black box theatre in a church basement on the edge of the Soulard neighborhood, another of St. Louis' hottest cultural areas. The St. Marcus Theatre had been around for about five years and until then had been the home of mostly gay-themed work. New Line became the third resident company to occupy the space, sharing it with Joan Lipkin's That Uppity Theatre Company and with Chris Jackson, a local writer who produced his own gay-themed musicals there.

The only drawback of New Line's new home was that the air conditioning broke down the week before their first show, *Assassins,* opened and the entire run of the show played in windowless ninety-degree June heat. Even later on, after the air conditioning was fixed, summer shows were always a challenge. The air conditioning was too loud to run during the performances, so New Line had to cool the theatre down to sixty degrees before the house opened, let it warm up during Act I, turn the AC back on during intermission, and then feel the heat return during Act II. Shows without intermissions, like *Assassins* and *Pippin,* and longer shows, like *Sweeney Todd*, could be murder. It wasn't until the last few shows at the St. Marcus that New Line finally figured out how to strategically place fans around the theatre to keep audiences comfortable while the show played.

New Line's first show at the St. Marcus closed the company's third season. Stephen Sondheim's brilliantly subversive *Assassins* was a funny, quirky, ultimately chilling musical which turned the spotlight on the men and women who have tried to kill U.S. presidents. Bob Wilcox of *The Riverfront Times* called the production "ambitious, fascinating work." Steve Allen said on KFUO radio that the production "strives for perfection in every aspect." *Assassins* was the first of the kind of musicals that would soon define New Line—dark, confrontational, sexual, political, and frequently controversial.

The 1994-95 season opened with the darkly sexual, deliciously cynical *Pippin*, the musical-within-a-musical focusing on a self-absorbed young man looking for total fulfillment. As New Line would do over and over again, it stripped *Pippin* down to its essentials—sex, war, politics, and religion—and discarded all the extra trappings Broadway had imposed on this wonderful, underrated show. The focus was returned to the brilliantly constructed script and score, the psychology, the subtext, the humor, the *truth* of the story. And it worked. All the people who had always believed the show wasn't strong enough to stand on its own, without original director Bob Fosse's razzle dazzle, were proved wrong. Harry Weber wrote in *The Riverfront Times*, "*Pippin* seems to me to be New Line's slickest production to date—skilled cast, excellent technical work, and polished vision." Bob Wilcox, also of *The Riverfront Times*, said "If you like musical theatre that goes for the guts, head for the St. Marcus Theatre…where New Line's *Pippin* runs."

The season continued with the world premiere of Scott Miller's third original show for New Line, the vampire musical *In the Blood*, which told of an unlikely romance between a gay hematologist and the vampire Zachary Church. Set in the early era of AIDS, it asked question about responsibility and compromises in the face of this horrific pandemic. Bob Wilcox said, in *The Riverfront Times*, that *In the Blood* was "the best score [Scott Miller]'s done for a show."

In the Blood received mixed reviews, but it spawned one of New Line's most popular songs, the ten minute "Tale of Zachary Church," which was included on a CD of songs from gay-themed musicals and has been performed in two subsequent New Line concerts. *In the Blood* also marked the first time New Line did a public reading of a work in progress before it was produced. Because that reading was such a success and so valuable in the development of the show, New Line decided to sponsor other readings over the years, including two shows by St. Louis writer and composer Al Fisher, *All About Steve* and *Switch*.

It was in 1995 that Broadway composer Jerry Herman (*Hello, Dolly!*, *Mame*, *La Cage aux Folles*) joined Stephen Sondheim as an honorary member of the New Line board.

The 1995-96 season opened with Sondheim's marriage musical *Company*, the ground-breaking 1970 concept musical about the complexity of human relationships in our modern world. It received mixed reviews. Woefully underestimating New Line's audiences, Susan Wells wrote in the *West End Word*, "Perhaps giving the audience too much to notice and think about can be dangerous."

The second show of the season was *Out on Broadway*, an evening of theatre songs performed from a gay perspective. With a single piano onstage and a cast of five men, this show became one of New Line's biggest hits. Mike Isaacson, of *The Riverfront Times*, called the show "a sweetly rewarding and happy surprise." It was so popular that, though the original run could not be extended, the show was brought back "by popular demand" later that year, after the regular season was over. A cast album was recorded and was scheduled to be released, but it ended up sitting on the shelf for four years before a major label finally picked it up and released it.

Though New Line's shows had sometimes been controversial enough to induce occasional, individual walk-outs, *Out on Broadway* hit a nerve. Anonymous extremists calling themselves "The Committee of Concern" sent letters to all of New Line's government funders demanding that the funders cancel the show (which, of course, was not within their authority), and that New Line's funding be terminated for producing this "fraudulent, deceitful, and highly illegal" show. They called the show's premise "God-playing hogwash." Luckily, some funders ignored the letters; others were mildly amused. The "Committee" also sent letters to the licensing agents who represent the musicals from which *Out on Broadway* used songs. But again, after phone calls to New Line to confirm the truth, the agents ignored the letters.

The season closed with New Line's most ambitious production to date, Sondheim's epic tragedy *Sweeney Todd*. Produced on a mammoth scale on Broadway in 1979, Sondheim said he had always intended the show to be a small chamber musical. So New Line created an intimate, environmental production, placing the action of the story all over the small St. Marcus Theatre. With three stages, two of which had revolving platforms, with street scenes played in the theatre's aisles, a cast of only thirteen, and an audience seating about a hundred, the production's intimacy made the story of madness, murder, and cannibalism even scarier, funnier, and a lot more disturbing. Judith Newmark wrote in *The St. Louis Post-Dispatch*, "To be honest, I've seen *Sweeney Todd* before and never liked it. But this production made me consider it from a different perspective; I appreciate that." For years after, she used New Line's *Sweeney* as an example of the value of small venues.

Continuing the Sondheim streak, New Line opened the 1996-97 season with the St. Louis premiere of Sondheim's dark, unconventional love story *Passion*. Though most musicals end with a Happily Ever After, *Passion* begins with the Happily Ever After and then deconstructs it, as it tells the story of a beautiful married woman who is having an affair with a handsome soldier, who in turn is the object of an ugly, dying woman's obsession. True to its title, this is not a show about love; it is about passion, sometimes exciting, sometimes dangerous, always extreme. It was a hit with audiences and critics. Gerry Kowarsky said in *The Post-Dispatch* that "the New Line Theatre production of *Passion* is a triumph for director Scott Miller and his company."

The season continued with one of the strangest shows New Line had produced up to that point, *Jacques Brel is Alive and Well and Living in Paris*, an abstract concept musical, an evening of songs by the Belgian-French coffee house singer-songwriter Jacques Brel. The show had been a major hit off-Broadway in the late 1960s and became a cult favorite. *Brel* is not a "normal" musical, but it is more than just a revue. Perhaps it is most accurately an "abstract" musical, a label that fit equally well a show New Line would produce several years later, *Songs for a New World*. *Brel* is a one-man show, but a one-man show in which four actors play that man, giving voice to one man's thoughts, passions, loves, fears, and politics. It was a remarkable experience for the cast bringing this incredible work to life, and they found it great fun playing it night after night for the hard-core Brel fans who came from all over the country to see the rarely produced show.

The season closed with the St. Louis premiere of the gay-themed musical *The Ballad of Little Mikey*, by Los Angeles writer-composer Mark Savage. *Mikey* is a warm, funny, thought-provoking show about the coming of age of a gay activist in the late 1970s and the parallel coming of age of the gay community and gay politics. In reviewing *Mikey*, Steve Callahan said on KDHX radio that "Scott Miller and his New Line Theatre continue to bring St. Louis challenging, refreshing musical theatre that you simply can't see anywhere else."

The 1997-98 season began with another concert of Stephen Sondheim's theatre songs, this time called *Extreme Sondheim*, an evening of Sondheim's saddest, funniest, most complex, most emotional, and most difficult songs, all brought together in one happily overwhelming show. In the *St. Louis Post-Dispatch,* Judith Newmark wrote, "At New Line Theatre, where *Extreme Sondheim* is now playing, comedy carries the day. The show sparkles…"

Unexpectedly, it provided one of the scariest moments in New Line's history. After confirming that ASCAP, the songwriter's service organization, could grant New Line the performance rights for this concert, New Line paid the fee and went into rehearsal. Because Sondheim is an honorary member of the New Line board, he was one of many people in New York who received the New Line newsletter announcing the show about two weeks before the show opened. One week before opening night, New Line received a phone call from Sondheim's licensing agent who said that ASCAP could not actually grant those rights and that the production would not be allowed to go on. After many letters and lots of begging, Sondheim himself stepped in and graciously gave permission for the show to open as planned. The permission finally came the day before the show was scheduled to open. Director Scott Miller didn't tell the cast until after the problem had been resolved.

The season continued with something rare in musical theatre and completely new for New Line. The company held an international competition for one-act musicals, a very unusual form in musical theatre. After inquires from around the world and twenty-eight submissions from across the United States, New Line chose *Woman with Pocketbook*, by a team of writers from New York and New Jersey, Annie Kessler, Libby Saines, and Jeff Blumenkrantz. It was a charming thirty-minute musical about a woman who dies and goes to heaven but can't get in because she refuses to give up her beloved purse, a deal-breaker for the heavenly gatekeeper. After appeals from her dead husband, her dead mother, and God himself, the title character Doris is sent back to earth as a statue (with the title "Woman with Pocketbook"), where she finally relents and sings a tearful love song to her purse before relinquishing it and returning to heaven.

Sharing the stage in this evening of one-acts was William Finn's off-Broadway musical *March of the Falsettos*, a show that later formed one-half of the Broadway musical *Falsettos*. *March of the Falsettos* is a dark comedy about a gay man who leaves his wife and son for his male lover while his psychiatrist moves in on the ex-wife. Bob Wilcox, of *The Riverfront Times*, said, "New Line Theatre's current production of *Falsettos* may be the best work this company has done." In *The Post-Dispatch*, Gerry Kowarsky, called the production, "angry, challenging work."

The season ended with a show New Line had already produced once before, Stephen Sondheim and John Weidman's brilliant off-Broadway musical *Assassins*. Last produced by New Line four years earlier, this time it was staged in the round, with an audience barely three feet from the stage, making the already confrontational, in-your-face musical even more intense and disturbing, not to mention a lot funnier. This staging also underlined an important theme of the show—that these assassins aren't all that different from normal, everyday men and women—by forcing the audience to watch each other across the stage, setting each scene against a backdrop of "ordinary people." The production sold out almost every performance. Mike Isaacson, in *The Riverfront Times*, said, "New Line Theatre's frequently thrilling *Assassins* sets a new standard for the St. Marcus Theatre, and it easily ranks as one of the finest works ever produced there."

In the summer of 1998, New Line set out on a new adventure. The company created an alter-ego, Out of Line Productions, to produce David Dillon's non-musical, gay-themed comedy *Party*, which had been a major hit in Chicago, Los Angeles, off-Broadway, and elsewhere. *Party* was certainly controversial because it included full male nudity, but it also proved to be the most financially successful show New Line had ever produced. Gerry Kowarsky said in the *Post-Dispatch* that "*Party* is consistently amusing and frequently hilarious."

The 1998-99 season began with what may be the most exhilarating, most unusual show New Line has ever produced, Jason Robert Brown's brilliant off-Broadway musical *Songs for a New World*, a small, four-actor, abstract musical that had played for a limited run in New York.

The show's cast album brought it to the attention of New Line's artistic director, and it proved to be one of the most challenging shows New Line ever produced and, for the people who worked on it, definitely the most satisfying and the most memorable. *Songs for a New World* is a collection of songs dramatizing those moments in life when everything's fine and suddenly disaster strikes; your life crumbles and you find yourself in a whole new world, where the old rules no longer apply. Each song dealt with such a moment—a divorce, a possible suicide, an unexpected pregnancy, a lost job, imprisonment. Mike Isaacson of *The Riverfront Times*, called the production "a true theatrical gem" and "a truly cherished memory."

But, forced to open on Halloween, *Songs for a New World* suffered the worst opening weekend attendance in New Line history. On opening night, there were twelve people in the audience, six of whom were critics. But despite the slow start, the crowds increased over the three-week run and by the end, there were full houses. Still, the bad timing and low attendance created New Line's first budget deficit, with which the company would grapple for three years before it was retired.

The season continued with another unusual production, this time the classic Broadway musical *Camelot*. It was unusual for two reasons. First, *Camelot* isn't the kind of show New Line produces; it's an old, mainstream musical and the first show New Line ever produced that audiences could easily see on other St. Louis stages. It was also unusual because even though *Camelot* is known as a big, old-fashioned musical, New Line bucked convention and staged it with a cast of thirteen, focusing not on spectacle and fancy costumes, but instead on psychology and character, and the well-known tragic love triangle of Arthur, Guenevere, and Lancelot. Judy Newmark said in the *St. Louis Post-Dispatch*, "This show does not look, sound, or feel like any other *Camelot* [but]…this stripped down version has a lot going for it." Steve Callahan said on KDHX radio that "its command of our attention is unfailing." It sold out much of its run.

The season ended with an environmental production of Stephen Sondheim's *Into the Woods*, for which New Line turned the entire St. Marcus Theatre into a forest. The action of the show played all around and throughout the audience, actually placing the audience there in the woods along with Red Riding Hood, Cinderella, Jack, and the Baker and his Wife. Again, almost every performance sold out, and Bob Wilcox of *The Riverfront Times* called the show "New Line's finest production yet."

In August 1999, Out of Line Productions returned for another project, this time for *Head Games*, the first non-musical play artistic director Scott Miller had written. *Head Games* is a satire of shows like *Party*, and also of the people who produce shows like *Party* and the people who go to see shows like *Party*. The play raised questions about gay theatre, about commercialism in theatre, about audiences, and about obscenity and nudity in the theatre, all with a wicked sense of humor. Gerry Kowarsky wrote in the *St. Louis Post-Dispatch*, "The funniest moment in *Head Games* occurs when a character questions the artistic integrity of a director who plans to stage a play with gratuitous nudity. The irony is that the actor expressing these sentiments is gratuitously nude." Harry Weber wrote in *The Riverfront Times*, "Miller takes *Head Games* well beyond the dick-play genre. His director's program note and the piece in last week's *RFT* tell the audience in advance what Miller is going to do, but it's like a magician's explaining a trick before he performs it and still amazing his spectators."

Quite a few of New Line's regular performers were itching to do another concert, so in September of 1999, the company produced a one-night-only concert of songs from shows New Line had produced, featuring fourteen of New Line's greatest performers all together, recreating their greatest moments. The evening was called *A New Line Songbook*.

The 1999-2000 season officially opened in November with the St. Louis premiere of another remarkable work, Adam Guettel's off-Broadway masterpiece *Floyd Collins*, a show that legendary Broadway composer Stephen Sondheim called the best musical of the last twenty-five years. Telling the true story of a man trapped in a Kentucky cave in 1925, it wowed audiences and sold out most performances. Judith Newmark wrote in *The St. Louis Post-Dispatch*, "New Line Theatre...continues the hot streak that began last season with *Camelot* and *Into the Woods*. Scott Miller's productions always are small in scale, but the imaginative scope of these recent shows has impressive depth."

With internal political problems brewing in the St. Marcus church, the future of the theatre downstairs looked precarious. After numerous meetings, promises, and too many unexpected twists, the church announced in a decision covered by the press that it would be closing the theatre in July at the end of the 1999-2000 season. It was a major setback not only for the companies involved, but also for the theatre community at large and the gay community in St. Louis. But the St. Marcus story was not over.

New Line's season continued with its first sequel, *Out on Broadway 2000*, another installment of 1996's *Out on Broadway*, again taking theatre songs and presenting them from a gay perspective. The show included songs from *Rent, Yentl, Fiddler on the Roof, Working, Grease, Little Shop of Horrors, Annie Get Your Gun, Guys and Dolls, Ballroom, Aspects of Love, Faust, Cabaret, South Pacific, Jesus Christ Superstar, Closer Than Ever, Woman of the Year, Follies, Ragtime, A New Brain*, and other shows. Four of the five cast members from the original production came back for the sequel. And just at that time, a major record label in New York finally agreed to release the 1996 *Out on Broadway* cast album. Judith Newmark wrote in *The Post-Dispatch*, "At least the quirky little [St. Marcus] theater is going out in style."

But during the run of *Out on Broadway 2000*, church members began sabotaging the show, tearing down lighting cables, calling city inspectors to the theatre, threatening to call police if wine was served at an opening night reception. After eleven years, the theatre in their basement had become a battleground. Only with the help of sympathetic city officials was the show allowed to finish its run. But the church announced they would break their promise to keep the theatre open until the end of the season; they would shut it down when *Out on Broadway 2000* closed. Within a few days of the show's last performance, the stage and technical booth had been destroyed. A long and distinguished history of St. Louis theatre had ended.

So New Line was homeless and still had another show scheduled to close the season. The local press jumped on the story, but none of the major local arts institutions stepped up to the plate to help out the three companies thrown out of the St. Marcus. Luckily, at the last minute, New Line made a deal with Washington University to use their black box theatre for the last show of the season, *Hair*. But it was a one-time-only deal.

So, a mere two weeks before *Hair* was scheduled to open, New Line had finally found a temporary home. The show opened to the most enthusiastic audiences New Line had ever encountered, people coming from around the country to see the show, dozens of strangers getting up to dance at the end of each performance, people crying, embracing cast members. Just as each cast of *Hair* over the years has picked a tribe name, the New Line cast became the Osage Tribe and formed an intense bond. The production sold out all but two performances. Judith Newmark, of the *St. Louis Post-Dispatch*, called it "a gripping production" and "a stunning depiction of how immediate the threat felt to people a world away from the war."

But New Line was still homeless.

The Sheldon Concert Hall, one of the most acoustically perfect concert halls in the country, invited New Line to bring a concert to their Notes from Home Series, a series showcasing local talent. So New Line opened its tenth season with *A New Line Cabaret*, again recreating some of New Line's most amazing moments with a cast of fifteen of New Line's all-stars, a fitting way to begin New Line's tenth anniversary season.

HotHouse Theatre Company, another local company, approached New Line about sharing their space, a black box theatre downtown called the ArtLoft Theatre. Along with the property's owners, represented by Tim Boyle, they welcomed New Line into its new permanent home. The tenth season was announced, including *Cabaret*, Stephen Sondheim's *Anyone Can Whistle*, and a re-mounting of *Hair*, this time for an open-ended run. Finally, New Line had a home again—just in time to finish its tenth season.

Cabaret was an unqualified hit, selling out nearly every show and receiving raves from the critics. In *The Post-Dispatch*, Judith Newmark called it "one of the most powerful productions that Miller's company, New Line Theatre, has ever staged." Steve Callahan, of KDHX-FM, called it "the most remarkable production to hit St. Louis this season…And it's one of the best things I've seen the New Line Theatre do." Gerry Kowarsky, also of *The Post-Dispatch*, called it "a must-see for anyone who is interested in theatre in St. Louis."

Anyone Can Whistle, as the New Liners expected, evoked wildly mixed reactions. Audiences for the first couple performances were unresponsive almost to the point of hostility, but by the third or fourth show, audiences seemed to love the show's bizarre, confrontational, absurdist comedy, and despite mixed reviews and very little name recognition, more than half the run sold out. But the critics just didn't get it. Maybe they wanted it to be something other than what it was. Maybe they were judging it by rules that just didn't apply to *Whistle*. Maybe they'd never seen an absurdist musical before and didn't know how to review one. Whatever the reasons, the kindest reviewers dismissed the show but complimented the production. The less kind reviewers were downright mean. Judith Newmark said in the *Post-Dispatch*, "The best reason to see *Anyone Can Whistle*…is simple. You're not likely to get another chance." In *The Riverfront Times*, Cliff Froehlich said, "Putting it in the kindest terms, New Line Theatre's *Anyone Can Whistle* has more historical interest than aesthetic worth."

Joe Pollack, of KWMU-FM, put it most directly: "Stephen Sondheim is one of the great musical theatre composers and lyricists of the 20th century, but even the best have early mistakes to overcome. Sometime these mistakes are quietly shelved, but with Scott Miller on hand, it isn't likely for Sondheim."

Excitement had been building around the remounting of New Line's production of *Hair*, and six new cast members joined the "tribe" to replace others who couldn't return. *American Theatre* magazine, the top professional theatre magazine in the world, sent a writer from New York to St. Louis to see the show and interview the New Liners. That writer, Allison Xantha Miller, later wrote that the show's finale was "almost unbearably emotional." And Michael Butler, who produced the original Broadway production of *Hair* in 1968, flew out from Los Angeles just to see New Line's production. He later called it "masterful."

New Line still enjoys unprecedented success, and the national press, the local press, and audiences from throughout the region continue to show New Line the kind of support that is very rare for an alternative theatre company. As New Line begins its eleventh season, three more amazing productions are on tap: *The Cradle Will Rock*, running in rotating repertory with HotHouse Theatre Company's production of *It's All True*, a play about the creation of *Cradle*; the St. Louis premiere of *A New Brain*; and the Broadway mega-hit *Chicago*. And Miller is negotiating rights for *Bat Boy*, *Reefer Madness*, *Urinetown*, and other nonconformist musicals for future seasons.

Few companies can sustain a policy of producing alternative work, new work, and controversial work, and still survive. Fewer still end up thriving. Though most companies wait till the twenty-fifth anniversary to create a commemorative book, New Line's journey has been exciting enough, improbable enough, and enough of a testament to the intelligence and sophistication of Midwest audiences and artists, that it seems appropriate to create this tenth anniversary volume, to honor the hundreds of artists and the tens of thousands of audience members who have made New Line a success, and who have proven once and for all, that producing *The Sound of Music* and *Hello, Dolly!* is not the only way for a company to be financially stable and commercially viable. Audiences *don't* only want what they know. They want what's good. They want what's exciting. They want an adventure.

And the adventure continues...

Remembering the First Ten Years

♦

Congratulations to New Line Theatre, and thanks from everybody who cares about musicals for its continued support and exploration.
—Stephen Sondheim
Broadway composer/lyricist and
Honorary New Line board member

    I have a hard time believing some of the dates when I look at a full list of New Line Theatre's productions. Was *Sweeney Todd* really done in 1995, *Passion* in 1996, *Assassins* in both 1994 and 1998? My memories of these shows and others are more vivid than these dates would suggest.
    The lesson of New Line is that ideas contribute more to memorable theater than money. The thought that goes into New Line productions has always made up for the lack of funds for technical resources.
    New Line is a theater of ideas in two ways. First, artistic director Scott Miller selects shows that have ideas. He has little patience with the notion that musical theater is not serious theater. I have e-mails to prove it. At New Line, words and music have equal importance in communicating a significant message. If anything, the presence of music makes the theater more powerful and, therefore, more serious.
    Second, Scott has ideas about the shows he selects. I do not agree with all of Scott's interpretations, but they are always thought-provoking and fully worked out. Some directors write a few paragraphs of program notes about the shows they do. Scott writes comprehensive

twenty-or thirty-page essays that treat musicals with the respect they deserve but seldom receive.

New Line productions are nothing if not thoroughly researched. Scott sends his essays to reviewers in advance, and reading them before the show has always enhanced my experience. The essay on *Hair* was particularly impressive. Scott is too young to remember the late 60s and early 70s, but his research led him to an interpretation that rang true to someone who lived through that period. Happily, his insights carried over from the page to the stage.

Scott's insights are musical as well as verbal. He is an outstanding accompanist because he is not simply an accompanist. His full understanding of the show is reflected in the music he plays as well as the action he directs.

Ten years of New Line is an occasion to celebrate. Let there be many more years and celebrations.

—Gerry Kowarsky
reviewer, *St. Louis Post-Dispatch*

Jerzy Grotowski, the great Polish director and drama theorist who articulated the advantages of economically "poor theater," gave himself one heck of a hard sell.

Nobody wants to be poor. Nobody in theater does, that's for sure. Think of the sets, of the costumes, of the paltry actors' salaries that a little bit of money could buy. "Poor theater" is not an ambition for Scott Miller. Just look at the lapel button on his old leather jacket. It sums up the artistic director's endless plight: "I need money bad."

No doubt, it tells the truth—but not the whole truth. The economic hardship that has dogged New Line for all of its ten years has also helped Miller shape the lean, brainy production style that distinguishes New Line's work at its best—a style that makes the audience complicit in the creation of every show. Imagination, on the both sides of the footlights, is the one inexhaustible resource Miller has at his disposal, and he's never been too shy to mine it.

His techniques—small casts (even for shows that usually have big ones), costumes and scenery that are evocative rather than lush, minimal instrumentation—show off new material with a frank economy that allows work to speak for itself. "Here I am, and I bet you've never seen me before," says a New Line production of something like *Floyd Collins* or *Out on Broadway*. "Well, you'll see me now, and I won't be hiding behind a lot of hoopla. Let me know what you think."

But Miller, who loves and is a diligent student of historic musical theater, has left his most telling marks with stripped-down stagings of shows that the audience generally has seen before, in very different, and generally more affluent, contexts. New Line's distinctive style—the bare-bones look and sound, the intimate staging necessitated by small, relatively inexpensive theaters—changes the audience's perspective on the production. The change starts in physical terms. It doesn't necessarily end there.

Consider a few examples.

—With the performers practically in the audience's lap, Stephen Sondheim's *Sweeney Todd* loses its uneasy connection to mainstream musical theater and discovers its rightful legacy, the highly political, presentational style associated with Bertolt Brecht and Kurt Weill.

—Miller scales another Sondheim show, *Into the Woods*, down to nursery-sized proportions that suit both the tiny St. Marcus house and the fairy-tale protagonists, enhancing the musical's message of loss and longing.

—Lerner and Loewe's *Camelot*, performed by a cast of thirteen (the usual is around thirty-five), holds onto the tragic triangle at its core with three actors who command the stage, now that it's not so crowded.

—The rarely-revived agit-prop musical, *The Cradle Will Rock*, relies, like *Sweeney Todd*, on a strongly presentational style. In this case, the actors never even get on the stage. But the theater is intimate enough to allow the audience to follow them easily as they deliver Marc Blitzstein's driving political message.

Two of New Line's most successful productions, *Cabaret* and *Hair*, can't have come as surprises to their audience. Both were big Broadway hits; both have been made into movies. Productions like these raise a reasonable question: Why bother?

Miller, however, has a good answer: Bother because, on a different scale, without the luxurious trappings that money can buy, these shows say something worth bothering about. *Hair*, with its profoundly American vision of a tie-dyed City upon a Hill, and *Cabaret*, a seedy exploration of a world on the brink of calamity, are shows that it takes nerve to get close to. Miller's nerve is strong enough for the audience to rely on. New Line doesn't do "feel-good" shows; it does "feel-something" shows, a tougher and smarter choice.

Maybe New Line does need money. But not too much—not when its lack has served it, and its audience, so well.

—Judy Newmark
senior critic, *St. Louis Post-Dispatch*

Ten years of a small theatre company is a wondrous thing. Located in the buckle of the Bible Belt, it is miraculous. It has been my pleasure to watch New Line Theatre survive and even thrive over the past decade. The quality of the performances has steadily improved as more and more talented local actors have discovered the artistic opportunities and freedom a small maverick company can offer.

And while nobody achieves anything alone in the theatre, so much of New Line's success has been accomplished through the vision and dedication of its artistic director, Scott Miller. Ever the optimist, Scott sees possibilities in the most reduced circumstances. Given the poles at the St. Marcus Theatre, he dressed them up and made them part of the set. No matter that he was in the basement of a church; he made bold use of the space and asked audiences to join him on a journey of imagination.

I love Scott Miller. I loved sharing space with him at the St. Marcus while he rehearsed upstairs and we had tech rehearsals downstairs. I loved hearing his infectious laugh wafting down as he worked with his cast who were clearly having a ball. Most of all, I love how he loves musicals and dedicates so much of his life to them. And because he does, we reap the benefit of his hard work.

Scott Miller and New Line are good for St. Louis and good for the American theatre. My thanks and congratulations to Scott, his hardworking board of directors, and all the actors, designers, tech staff, and volunteers who helped support this company that is small on budget, but big on ambition and heart.

I lift my glass and toast to another ten years.

—Joan Lipkin
Artistic Director
That Uppity Theatre Company

All I want is to work hard. I want to be challenged, I want to surprise myself, scare myself, chase after something. Since college, I'd worked with four companies who were fun to work with and put on quality theatre productions, yet they all lacked something. Simply put, they lacked Scott Miller. He has vision, he has knowledge and experience, and certainly confidence and flair. When it comes down to it, however, none of that matters if you don't have two things. First, you have to passionately believe in the value of what you're doing. Scott believes. Trust me, to the core of his being, he believes. Second, you have to be able to enkindle the same tempestuousness in everyone else involved. Honestly, I couldn't begin to tell you how he does this so well. He's not a leader like Vince Lombardi or Patton or certainly not like Orson Wells. Scott, and therefore New Line Theatre, is the embodiment of complete unblemished love, even lust, for theatre. This sort of unfettered ardor attracts an unprecedented collection of talent to the company. I can't count on both hands the number of actors, musicians and technicians who have commented on this fact. You simply have to sit back in awe at the collection of talent that surrounds you when you work in a New Line Theatre production. This is the one-two punch of New Line Theatre. Not only do you wish to work with Scott and the challenging material he produces, but the skill level of the ensemble pushes every production beyond the talents of any single individual. It's a pleasure to experience. I've all but resigned myself to working solely with New Line Theatre. It's so many things. It's the professionalism. It's the material. It's the fear of the material. It's the successes. The failures. The laughs. We laugh a lot. We laugh, we learn, we discover, and all the while, we never stop the exploring and the working. I'm proud to be a part of the New Line group, to be a New Liner. I'm sure there are some who like theatre to be about the fun, but it's twice the fun when it's about the theatre. Scott Miller and his New Line Theatre are what theatre is all about.

—Troy Schnider, New Line actor since 1998

The year was 1996 and I hadn't set foot on a stage for six years. Then out of the blue I got a call from Cindy Duggan telling me that a theatre company named New Line was looking for someone to play Judge Turpin in their upcoming production of *Sweeney Todd*. They had had no luck in finding someone to play the part during the audition process, so they talked about actors who could play an old fart and somehow my name came up.

I am not a musical theatre actor, I knew very little about *Sweeney Todd* and even less about New Line Theatre. So, like an idiot, I told Cindy I would meet this Scott Miller person and audition for him. I got the part.

When I arrived at the St. Marcus church for my first rehearsal, I had no idea what to expect. In retrospect, I can honestly say that heaven and hell *do* exist and they shared the same space in the basement of that church. The quality of the shows produced there were the heavenly part, the conditions, especially in the summer, were hell.

As I stated before, I had not done any kind of stage work for six years. I thought a little musical in a church basement would be easy. No big sets, costumes or orchestra to deal with. I did, however, have to deal with a Sondheim show and Scott Miller.

Both scared the heck out of me. My fear of Sondheim was justified because *Sweeney Todd* was the closest thing to opera I had ever tried. My fear of Scott turned into respect. He knew what he was doing. Scott had cast the show with some of the most amazing performers I had ever worked with.

One thing I wasn't prepared for was Scott's enthusiastic use of colorful language. He would curse more in one night than an entire ship of sailors with the clap taking a leak at the same time. The fact that we were in a church basement didn't seem to bother him. I kept waiting for lightning to strike. Heck, I'm not a prude. In fact, I avoid going to church religiously. But as the son of a Southern Baptist preacher, I was taught that cussing, especially in a church, was not a good thing.

Then, during one rehearsal that wasn't going too well, (the cast was having trouble with the song "God That's Good"), Cindy and I read Scott the riot act. We told him that we needed to work on the song and get it right before we moved on. I may have said a couple of bad words during the exchange. Scott sort of smiled and then took the time to review the song with us. I thought that I had made an enemy and would never work at New Line again.

Sweeney Todd opened and it was an incredible show. The audiences and critics loved it. I've since been involved with several other New Line shows that were as great if not better. If you've seen a New Line show, you've seen what theatre can and should be. If you've ever been in a New Line show, I hope you know how lucky you are. I know I do.

By the way, we never got the song "God That's Good" exactly right during the run of *Sweeney*.

—Steven R. Johnson
New Line actor since 1996

Long before I had heard of New Line Theatre, I was a counselor for a summer church camp near Steelville, Missouri. It was there that I met a girl named Katie who was also a counselor for the Music, Art, and Drama week. So seven years later, I saw *Into the Woods* at New Line, and a couple of cast members I already knew asked me to come out with them afterwards. So I did, and as Fate would have it, I sat down next to a girl named Katie who had played Little Red Riding Hood in the show. She looked at me, and said, "Colin?" and a few choruses of "It's a Small World" ensued.

I spent my entire life singing in choirs and choruses, but never had any classical training in voice until college. When I left school, I went searching for a group that would help me grow as a performer, with people that would understand my "unnatural" preoccupation with the arts. One day, I saw an ad for the upcoming theatre season in St. Louis, and that New Line would be producing *Assassins*, which had long been one of my favorite shows. But I was still apprehensive about the audition, even questioning whether I should go at all. I made it (though I called in sick to do it), sang a song cold, and left without having said hardly a word to anyone. My doubt was still with me until I saw a bumper sticker on one of the cars that had arrived after me: I BRAKE FOR AUDITIONS. I knew then that I had found the right people.

Theatre creates a universal feeling among its family. Where else can two people almost recognize each other, talk for ten minutes about people that the other person never quite knows, mention show after show that the one or the other hasn't been in, and part ways having made a connection that neither one can quite define?

—Colin DeVaughan
New Line actor since 1998

As I enter college this year, I look back over my high school years in St. Louis. By all outward appearances they were pretty much a bust. I graduated with a poor grade point average, wasn't president of my drama club. Heck, I didn't even go to my senior prom. I didn't want to do what was expected of me, and I pursued what I was interested in, particularly musical theatre.

I am by no means the stereotypical musical theatre consumer. I'm a sloppy straight male who watches football every weekend. Yet from the moment I was first introduced to the work of Stephen Sondheim in the seventh grade I was hooked. This man was finding a true synthesis between music and drama, and layering it more deeply than I ever could've imagined. I wasted no time in purchasing anything I could find that had anything to do with Sondheim. My cast recording collection that started with a single copy of *Into the Woods* ballooned into a virtual library his work: everything from *Sweeney Todd* to *Do I Hear a Waltz?*

As much as I was enjoying listening to the CDs and discussing the music on the internet, I longed to see one of these brilliant shows performed. I got my wish when I met Scott Miller via e-mail, and he introduced me to St. Louis's own New Line Theatre. I dragged my parents to this church basement downtown to see *Passion*, and we were blown away.

So for the next few years I made Scott my mentor of sorts, and New Line was my classroom. I attended all the shows, read Scott's book, and e-mailed him with a myriad of questions on a regular basis. These experiences showed me new layers in my favorite Sondheim pieces, but also introduced me to composers besides Sondheim, from Jason Robert Brown to Lerner and Loewe.

My senior year of high school, I convinced Scott to take me on as an intern for New Line's fall show. They were doing *Floyd Collins* by Adam Guettel. Despite its popularity within the theatre circles I ran with, I wasn't into *Floyd* like I was some other shows. I was nervous.

As the process wore on, that nervousness passed away. Themes and songs I'd paid no attention to on CD proved breathtaking when brought to life. The people I worked with on the show were all amazingly talented, and it showed me, someone who'd never worked on anything but high school plays, what it really was to put on a professional caliber show.

With all that under my belt, here I am. A freshman at a rural college that until recently had a theatre department policy against musicals. I don't know if my knowledge of leitmotifs or internal rhyming is going to impress anybody here, or if I'm going to be able to have part in the first musical to grace our school's stage in a generation. What I do know is that through my work with New Line I learned more about the art form than I ever dreamed possible. Thanks.

—Kevin Corlett, directing intern for *Floyd Collins*, 1999
enthusiastic audience member since 1996

A Tribute to the Rock Musicals 2

◆

a world premiere
Featuring songs from *Hair, Godspell, Jesus Christ Superstar, Grease, Pippin, The Wiz, The Rocky Horror Show, Working, Evita, Dreamgirls, Joseph and the Amazing Technicolor Dreamcoat, Little Shop of Horrors, Cats, Chess, Miss Saigon*, and other shows
Conceived and Researched by Scott Miller
April 10-18, 1992
Center of Contemporary Arts, St. Louis

THE CAST
Vincent Paul Boyle, Ellen Buck, Kevin Collier, Michelle Collier, Holli Folk, Michael Kaiser, Steve Kutheis, Loren Madden, Brendan O'Malley, Eric Pendleton, Ray Proctor, Patrick Ryan, Daniel Sattel, Deborah Sharn, Linda Walsh, Keve Wilson,
and John Gerdes as "The Professor"

THE ARTISTIC STAFF
Directors—Scott Miller, Steve Kutheis
Music Director—Scott Miller
Additional Staging—Michelle Collier, Vincent Paul Boyle
Production Consultant—Sara Lee Hart
Technical Director—Amy Lanning
Sound—Greg Rosebrock

Set Painting—Amy Lanning
Set Coordination—Kevin Collier
Business Manager—Holli Folk

THE BAND
Piano—Scott Miller
Keyboard—Claudia Baskind
Lead Guitar—Jim Folk
Electric Guitar—Brendan O'Malley
Rhythm Guitar—Joe Hermann
Bass—Mike Monsey
Saxophone/Flute—Kelly Rogers
Percussion—Adam Kopff

DIRECTOR'S NOTES

Opera had supplied the world with popular music since the early 1700s. For two centuries, as late as the premiere of Puccini's *Madame Butterfly* in 1906, many of the tunes people hummed on the streets of Europe and America were from operas. But in America during the first decade of this century, the public's taste for popular music turned to the operettas of Sigmund Romberg, Rudolf Friml, Victor Herbert, and Gilbert & Sullivan.

Then the First World War suddenly turned public sentiment in this country against all things Germanic, including the operetta. America became tremendously isolationist, and for the first time, the "young Americans" took over the musical theatre—Cole Porter, George M. Cohan, Irving Berlin, the Gershwins, and a little later, Rodgers & Hart. The war gave them a chance they might never have gotten otherwise to have their shows produced, shows that were decidedly American in content, character, and pacing. By the end of the war, American popular music was coming largely from musical comedy. And the sounds of jazz were a big part it, thanks primarily to George Gershwin.

But the musical theatre had grown away from the well-written, integrated book. The scripts written for musicals during the teens and twenties were little more than glorified vaudeville sketches. In 1943, that trend was reversed with *Oklahoma!*. And with that reversal, the music of the stage also reversed and headed back toward a more serious and somewhat "classical" style, instead of continuing in the same direction as pop music—the sounds of jazz and the Big Bands.

By the early 1950s popular music and stage music had split. And rock and roll (which had evolved from jazz) took over popular music. Some of the "young Americans" from the 1920s and '30s were still writing theatre scores, but were no longer the ones writing songs for the radio. The people who were writing for the stage didn't know rock and roll, and the new "young Americans" who were writing rock and roll songs didn't know stage music.

It wasn't until 1968 and the Broadway opening of *Hair* that theatre writers were brave enough to use rock and roll in a musical. And rock musicals grew more numerous and more sophisticated during the 1970s, including a few attempts at Rock Opera (*Jesus Christ Superstar, Tommy*), which worked artistically but didn't take hold because adults, who were the majority of theatre-goers, still didn't like rock music. The albums sold well, however, to the much younger record-buying public.

The mid-1970s was an exciting and experimental time for the rock musical. This decade turned out some remarkably successful shows, including *Grease*, the longest-running show in Broadway history until that time; *The Wiz*, a big step in the progress of the Black musical theatre; *The Rocky Horror Show*, a flop at first but a major cult classic soon after; and *A Chorus Line*, one of the most important and groundbreaking works of the musical theatre, and also the longest-running Broadway show in history. In fact, five of the ten longest running Broadway shows are now rock musicals. By this time, the teenagers of the 1950s and 60s had become adults, for whom the radio industry had created "adult rock" stations. And these new adult theatre-goers enjoyed theatre scores written in the style of rock and soft rock, the music they had grown up on.

The early 1980s saw great innovation. *Dreamgirls* employed almost continuous music for an entire show, very much in the tradition of melodrama and opera, and pioneered the use of cinematic scene changes—dissolves, fades, close-ups, etc.—a device used most recently by *City of Angels*. *Cats* carried the notion of the plotless, non-linear concept musical to the extreme and the gamble paid off. And by the end of the decade, a new form had appeared on Broadway, by way of London and Paris—the Pop Opera.

By the late 1980s and early 1990s, pop opera took hold in shows such as *Les Misérables, Chess,* and *Miss Saigon.* Pop opera used the structure of classical opera and the musical vocabulary of current popular music. It was the first time in almost a century that operas were being written in contemporary popular style, and it revitalized a stagnating musical theatre. For the first time since the rock operas of two decades earlier, songs from the stage were regularly crossing over to the radio and being recorded by pop singers, just as the show tunes of the Twenties and Thirties had.

The American musical comedy is still young as art forms go, less than one hundred years old (not counting its various precursors). And its first generation of creators have only recently died and left the field open to new voices, voices raised on the sounds of rock and roll. The musical theatre had begun to wither because it was so hard for new voices to be heard. But now that the old voices have gone, perhaps the musical theatre will return to the legacy from which it came—speaking to its audience through the sounds of today, uniquely contemporary, uniquely brash, uniquely American.

Author's Note: How can this be A Tribute to the Rock Musicals 2, *if it is New Line's first show? The reason this is number two is that the first* Tribute to the Rock Musicals *was done by many of the same people with CenterStage Theatre Company several years earlier.*

THE REVIEWS

"...the impressively—sometimes overwhelmingly—enthusiastic, talented, skilled, and well-trained cast and band made *A Tribute to the Rock Musicals 2*...a high-energy, highly entertaining evening."—Bob Wilcox, *The Riverfront Times*

REMEMBERING ROCK TRIB 2

I was 18 years old when I first encountered New Line Theatre and Scott Miller. My only theatrical experience up until then had been a production of *Guys and Dolls* at St. Louis University High School and a production of *Jesus Christ Superstar* at the Muny—both of which were chorus roles. I was a rock musician that had sung in bands since my younger years and was in love with *Superstar* for the incredible rock score. It blew me away.

One day I saw an advertisement for auditions of New Line's *Tribute to the Rock Musicals 2* and the *Superstar* logo jumped out at me. I ran home, put on my *Superstar* CD and searched for an audition piece. I decided on "Everything's Alright." I wanted to sing the part of Jesus.

Not having had much auditioning experience, I was very nervous when I arrived. It must have taken me half an hour to fill out the audition sheet. I sat there, afraid that I was going to humiliate myself, and almost wimped out several times. I somehow managed to muster up the courage to stay until my name was mispronounced and fumbled into the audition room.

When I walked in, there were two women and a guy, Scott, sitting behind a piano smiling. All were very friendly, but I was still nervous as hell. Scott began to play some ascending scales and asked me to sing along to get an idea of my range. Well, I totally choked. I couldn't find a pitch to save my life. Scott stopped and told me to relax. We started over and it was a little better, but certainly nothing I was proud of.

I prayed that he would at least let me sing my prepared piece so there might be some semblance of redemption for the audition. Luckily, he did and it went very well. He had me sing the Judas part as well as the Jesus part and kept mentioning to the other two women that we had found the guy that could sing "Pity the Child." I didn't know what the hell they were talking about, but it sure sounded promising. I left the audition feeling like I had accomplished something, although I didn't quite know what.

About a week later, I received a letter in the mail congratulating me and welcoming me to the cast of *Tribute to the Rock Musicals 2*. I was ecstatic! I was completely enthused until I looked at the enclosed song list. Scott didn't cast me to sing the one song they were doing from *Jesus Christ Superstar*—"Everything's Alright." Being as that was the sole reason I auditioned, I was pissed. I contemplated not doing the show, but as corny as this may sound, something told me to stick with it. I decided to try something new and just give it a shot.

That was one of the greatest decisions I've ever made in my life. Little did I know at the time, but I was about to embark on an eye-opening journey that would educate me, entertain me, and reveal an inner passion that even further enhanced anything I had experienced with music alone. *Rock Trib* was a revue that was designed to teach the audience about rock music and its evolution on the stage. It definitely accomplished that goal, but it also ROCKED! It was that combination of knowledge and entertainment that made me fall in love with New Line.

Since then, I have been a part of many, many New Line shows and have worked with some utterly amazing casts. I would like to thank Scott Miller from the bottom of my heart for his incredible vision and the countless bits of information and advice that he has shared with me over the years. I treasure every moment I've had with New Line.

—Dan Sattel

Looking back, *Rock Trib 2* was almost insanely ambitious, assembling in one evening some of the biggest show stoppers from rock and pop musicals of the last twenty-five years—and as New Line's very first show! The most ambitious—foolish?—part was including the Montage ("Hello Twelve, Hello Thirteen") from *A Chorus Line*, a seventeen-minute musical sequence that included some very difficult solo work and some ridiculously difficult ensemble work. But this was the most talented cast I had worked with up until this time, and I think by sheer force of will we pulled it off. We recreated one of the most amazing, most emotional, most exciting musical sequences in the history of musical theatre, and it worked. It was exciting as hell. I'll never forget the first performance. When we finished the number, and the actors slowly melted back into that famous silhouette on that famous line, as the band hit that final musical button, the audience went wild. Cheering, screaming, whooping. It was a portent of things to come for New Line—repeatedly jumping off metaphorical cliffs into the waiting arms of enthusiastic, adventurous audiences. I carry that moment with me forever, every time I wonder if we can pull off my latest folly, every time we start rehearsals for a *Sweeney Todd* or a *Passion* or a *Floyd Collins* and I think, "How on earth can we do this?" The answer is that I don't know *how*, but I know we *will*.

—Scott Miller

Attempting the Absurd

◆

a world premiere
Book, Music, and Lyrics by Scott Miller
July 17-18, 1992
Center of Contemporary Arts, St. Louis

THE CAST
Darcy Bowles—Jenni Ryan
Jason Christopher—Dan Guller
Mrs. Christopher—Rose Marie Nester
Chaz Williams—Kevin Collier
Danny Hooper—Charlie Robin
Alex Throttlebottom—Dan Sattel
Mary—Mara Hesed
Val—Catherine Edwards
Audrey—Amy Willard
The Playwright—Joel Hackbarth
Floyd the Cop—Peter Wilson
The Judge—Joel Hackbarth
Alison Goldstein
Amy McInerney
Susan Schloss
Emily Shavers

THE ARTISTIC STAFF
Directors—Scott Miller and Steve Kutheis
Music director—Scott Miller
Orchestrations and Conductor—John Gerdes
Set Designer—Steve Kutheis
Lighting Designer—Brian Joyal
Set Coordinator—Kevin Collier
Business Manager—Holli Folk

THE REVIEWS

"Miller has a nice sense of the ridiculous. He also shows a good feeling for whimsy and, most important, he has a deep and abiding love for classic American musicals. I liked the show better than I thought I would; it's collegiate, sometimes sophomoric, but there are moments of great charm."—Joe Pollack, *St. Louis Post Dispatch*

"About as good an evening of first-view musical comedy as I've seen for a while…Miller's book, music, and lyrics range widely, intelligently, unsentimentally, and wittily over familiar and unfamiliar territory."—Harry Weber, *The Riverfront Times*

REMEMBERING ATTEMPTING THE ABSURD

My first experience with New Line was working on *Attempting the Absurd* in the summer of 1992. *Absurd* is a quirky little musical about a guy who knows he's only a character in a musical ('I have only a sketchy memory of my past, I feel like everything I do is controlled by someone, somewhere behind a word processor, and I never go to the bathroom.'). I loved playing Jason. He was equally at home in his fictional world as in the real one. He moved through life knowing that someone else was pulling the strings. He was a paradox wrapped in a contradiction wrapped in a bright red shirt.

One of the toughest parts of the show for me came in the second act with a song called "Old Time Musicals." Scott, obviously in the throes of sophisticated artistry, started the song with Jason rattling off a list of about eighteen different musicals. Being the professional that I am, I expressed my concern about such a lyrical challenge: "Scott, I will never, ever, *ever* be able to memorize this crap!"

"Dan," said Scott with the certainty of one who would bet the life of his pet orangutan that he was right, "It's a list song. It'll take you a little longer to learn, but you'll remember it forever."

"Right," I countered, secretly sure that nobody had ever been more wrong than Scott Miller was at this very moment. So I worked on that masochistic list and, lo and behold, one day I noticed I was able to recite it without the script. Not only was the show as much fun for the audience as it was for the performers, but I didn't flub a single show from that list.

Well, here it is, almost ten years later, and guess what? "*Oklahoma, The Sound of Music, 42nd Street, South Pacific...*" Damn it. Scott was right. Good news for the orangutan. Happy Tenth, New Line!

—Dan Guller, "Jason"

It is the peculiar curse of the American Musical Theatre that it is never realistic. No matter how gritty and real Tony & Maria's Spanish Harlem or Tevye's Anatevka might be, it will never be realistic for them to break from spoken word into song. Bob Fosse solved this problem with the film version of *Cabaret* by using only the songs performed onstage at the Kit Kat Klub. But by eliminating the other songs, the show really stopped being a musical in the strictest sense. This problem was a constant topic of discussion among the musical theatre crowd at college. There must be a way, we decided, to get around it. And then, senior year, it struck me—if the characters *know* they're in a musical, then their singing is realistically motivated. *They sing because they are characters in a musical.* Of course, this then presented lots of new logistical and philosophical problems,

problems my roommate David Flores and I argued over for the entire school year. After graduation I set to work, and six years later, my aptly named *Attempting the Absurd* became a reality, and fittingly, as the second show of my new musical theatre company. Because it's so much *about* musical theatre—a parody, a deconstruction, a loving tribute—and because, in an odd way, it's the ultimate musical comedy, it will always be my favorite of the ten shows I've written. It's not my most sophisticated score or my most artfully built script, but it's awfully funny and it still makes me giggle. What more can I ask?

—Scott Miller, author, composer, director

Smokin' Santa

◆

a world premiere
Conceived by Scott Miller
December 3-4, 1992
Center of Contemporary Arts, St. Louis

THE CAST
Ellen Buck, Kevin Collier, Michelle Collier, Holli Folk, Holly Gulick, Chris Johnson, Steve Kutheis, Eric Pendleton, Keith Price, Dan Sattel, Deborah Sharn, Jeremy Sher, Linda Smith

THE ARTISTIC STAFF
Director/Pianist—Scott Miller
Lighting Designer—Steve Dohrmann

REMEMBERING SMOKIN' SANTA

I'm a Jew in a Christmas concert. Sure I've heard these songs before, but never the words. Not really. Caroling to me was dancing around the house like Mrs. Brady, and we didn't do that very often either. So I decided to open my mind and heart and just listen to the spirit of the music. That's when I heard Holli singing "Have Yourself a Merry Little Christmas" onstage. I was in the back of the house lacing up my Chuck Taylors when the sound hit me. A deep, velveteen alto with all the depth of an ocean. And the sentiment, not just the words, hit me in one vast wave. I started crying like a baby, uncontrollably like when cutting onions, and I *heard* the song. I really heard it. It's a beautiful song. And Holli's a beautiful woman. Wow, what a voice.

—Jeremy Sher

Smokin' Santa was an interesting experiment, our first foray into cabaret style theatre. It was an eclectic…no, let's be honest, a *bizarre* mix of traditional carols and pop songs, novelty numbers, parodies, and classical pieces, everything from "You're a Mean One, Mr. Grinch" to the eleventh movement of Bach's Magnificat in D Major (performed with a swing beat and sunglasses), to a parody number called "The Song About Hanukkah" written by my friend Dan Guller to the tune of "America" from *West Side Story*. The show also included one song I wrote called "The Christmas Tree Fell Over and Our House is Burning Down." But despite the generous amount of silliness, it was also a very personal show for me. In high school, we did a vespers concert every year at Christmas, put together by the greatest choral teacher I've ever encountered, Jim Buffalo. Jim retired a couple years after I graduated and the vespers concerts ended. *Smokin' Santa* was in part my personal tribute to Jim Buffalo, and I included several pieces from the vespers concerts, including a processional of carols he put together, the comedy song "Fruitcake," the Bach piece (though with my own twist), a fourteenth-century motet called "In Bethlehem," and Jim's own, gorgeous arrangements of "O Holy Night." I'm not sure it entirely succeeded as a theatre piece, but it meant a lot to me, and it taught me a lot about building revues.

—Scott Miller, director

A Tribute to the Musicals of Stephen Sondheim

◆

a world premiere
Featuring songs from *West Side Story, Gypsy, A Funny Thing Happened on the Way to the Forum, Evening Primrose, Company, Follies, A Little Night Music, The Frogs, Sweeney Todd, Merrily We Roll Along, Into the Woods, Sunday in the Park with George,* and *Assassins*
Music and Lyrics by Stephen Sondheim
Conceived and Researched by Scott Miller
March 19-27, 1993
Center of Contemporary Arts, St. Louis

THE CAST
Winona Black, Beth Boschert-Duello, Kevin Collier, Michelle Collier, Tracy Collins, Rose Marie Fischer, Alison Goldstein, Joel Hackbarth, Tim Kent, Steve Kutheis, Tracy Paul Muchesko, Keith Price, John T. Ricroft, Jeremy Sher, Renée Trudell

THE ARTISTIC STAFF
Director—Scott Miller
Assistant Director—Dan Guller
Additional Staging—Tim Kent
Production Consultant—Sara Lee Hart
Instrumental Music Director—Kurt Eichholz
Set Designer—John T. Ricroft

Lighting Designer—Steve Dohrmann
Costumer Coordinator—Tim Kent
Stage Manager—Amy Lanning
Business Manager—Holli Folk

THE BAND
Piano—Scott Miller
Keyboards—Chris Hegarty
Bass—Kurt Eichholz
Percussion—Adam Kopff

DIRECTOR'S NOTES

"Of all the artists who have tried to transform the Broadway musical since *Oklahoma!*, no one has been more persistent than the composer and lyricist Stephen Sondheim." (Frank Rich, *New York Times*). Few of his shows have been hits. Many have been controversial in one way or another. All of them have been interesting.

It's difficult to put together a sampling of his work for two reasons. First, there's an almost endless supply of interesting material to choose from. Second, it's hard to take his songs out of their original contexts. To merely sing his songs makes it hard to see how masterfully he weaves characterization and plot throughout his songs. For instance, "Send in the Clowns" is a beautiful song, in or out of its show. But when you know the singer is a fading actress, the show business metaphors take on new meaning. When you know the man she's singing to once wanted to marry her, but she wasn't ready, it's even more ironic that now when she's finally ready, he's found someone else. When you know the background, it hurts more when she sings:

> *Just when I'd stopped opening doors,*
> *Finally knowing the one that I wanted was yours,*
> *Making my entrance again with my usual flair,*
> *Sure of my lines, no one is there.*

"Pretty Women" becomes more than just a pretty song when you know that Sweeney Todd is shaving the corrupt Judge Turpin, waiting for the perfect moment to slit his throat. "It's Hot Up Here" is so much funnier when you know the singers are figures in a painting, doomed to spend all eternity in the same pose in the same spot with the same people. "I Remember" becomes much more touching when you know the girl singing it has lived her life in a department store, and can only barely remember the last time she saw the sky.

We realized as we rehearsed the show that we would be demanding a lot from our audiences with this material, that they wouldn't be able to just sit back and listen. These songs demand as much from the audience as from the performers. Sondheim proves with every project that the musical theatre doesn't have to be a place where you turn off your brain; it can be a place for high drama, dark comedy, social commentary, and thoughtful looks at the human condition.

With this tribute, we present songs that are more truly musical scenes. And so that you can experience the full power of these moments, we present them as they were written to be performed. Stephen Sondheim is a great composer and lyricist, but he is also a great innovator and a great maker of theatre. His work deserves no less.

So prepare yourself for a tour of some of the most important work in the musical theatre in the last thirty-five years, from 1957 and *West Side Story* through 1991 and the controversial *Assassins*. As Sondheim wrote for *Gypsy*: Curtain up, light the lights, We've got nothing to hit but the heights.

REMEMBERING A TRIBUTE TO SONDHEIM

I remember auditioning for New Line's *Tribute to Sondheim* back in 1993. I was nervous, and Scott was accompanying me on "Maria" from *West Side Story*. I can't remember who else was in there, but I kept thinking to myself, "You're an actor, not a singer, dummy, what are you doing this fo—" and that was my cue. What did I know? I'd listened to the music and practiced it a hundred times, but I had no idea what they were expecting. I don't know what I was thinking, but the first million and a half bars of the song were, as I remembered them from recordings, echoey and somewhat off in the distance, like voices floating around. "The most beautiful sound I ever heard…Maria (Maria, Maria, Maria…)." I thought, "Well, that part of the song must come from someone else, so I'll just breeze past that part in the audition and get to the good stuff." I mumbled those words, on key, mind you, but I mumbled them nonetheless. I thought Scott would just say OK and jump to the good stuff, but *NO*, he stayed true to the music, so I mumbled on, until he asked me what I was doing. Uh, singing the song, dummy, I wanted to say. But that would've hurt my chances, so I just started singing the lyrics the way they were intended to be sung. I got a part (not *that* part), and took the graciousness and gentleness of those auditioners with me on the next million and a half auditions, and I remember them all.

—Jeremy Sher

Stephen Sondheim was becoming an important part of New Line Theatre at this time. A few months before this Tribute, we'd held a celebrity auction and received autographed items from Julie Andrews, Jerry Herman, Hal Prince, Gwen Verdon, Elaine Strich, Raul Julia, Jim Lapine, Harnick and Bock, Kander and Ebb, Marvin Hamlisch, and many other Broadway stars. Stephen Sondheim sent us an autographed copy of the private, never released cast album (on LP) of his 1966 television musical *Evening Primrose*. And I was presumptuous enough, when I wrote to thank him, to also ask him for a cash donation. He sent one. I then thanked him for that and asked if he would be an honorary member of our board. He wrote back and said he would be delighted. Doing this concert of his songs was very special for me because of how incredibly kind he had been to this new, small company way out in St. Louis. And it became a kind of prologue to New Line's first ten years, as we would go on to produce his shows *Assassins* (twice), *Company, Sweeney Todd, Passion, Into the*

Woods, Anyone Can Whistle, and another Sondheim concert, *Extreme Sondheim.* In addition, when we put *Out on Broadway* together several years later, about a third of the show was Sondheim's songs. He has had more of an impact on New Line than any other theatre artist, and we couldn't be prouder to count him among our supporters.

—Scott Miller, director

A Tribute to the Dark Side 2

♦

a world premiere
Featuring songs from *Little Shop of Horrors, Grand Hotel, City of Angels, Guys and Dolls, Grease, Sweet Charity, Mack and Mabel, Chicago, Working, Show Boat, Dreamgirls, Company, Jesus Christ Superstar, Promises Promises, Les Misérables, Miss Saigon,*
and other shows
Conceived by Scott Miller
October 15-23, 1993
New City School Theatre, St. Louis

THE CAST
Beth Boschert-Duello, Kevin Collier, Michelle Collier, Tracy Collins, Rose Marie Fischer, Holly Gulick, Lisa Karpowicz, Tim Kent, Judy Kreisman, Mike Monsey, Keith Price, Dan Sattel
Johanna Schloss, Quenten Schumacher II, Darin Wood,
Paul Schankman as the Emcee

THE ARTISTIC STAFF
Directors—Scott Miller and Steve Kutheis
Music Director—Scott Miller
Technical Director and Lighting Designer—Steve Dohrmann
Costume Coordinator—Tim Kent
Stage Manager—Amy Lanning

Promotions Manager—Keith Price
Advertising Manager—Kevin Collier
Poster/Program Cover Design—Tracy Collins
Interior Program Design—Ron Crooks

THE BAND
Piano—Scott Miller
Keyboards—Chris Hegarty
Guitar/Bass—Kurt Eichholz

DIRECTOR'S NOTES

The history of the Dark Side in the musical theatre is a long one. Our survey tonight goes back as far as 1925's *No! No! Nanette!*, which was only dark in the most innocent way—supposed adultery that was (of course) just a misunderstanding. The first true musical tragedy was 1927's *Show Boat*, which presented real people in difficult real life situations—racism, marriage to an alcoholic and compulsive gambler, single parenting—but *Show Boat* turned out to be a fluke, and it wasn't until 1943's *Oklahoma!* that a new trend really began.

Then in the 1950s, director/choreographer Bob Fosse arrived, the Grand Master of Dark, and creator of many dark works, including *Sweet Charity, Chicago, Pippin*, and the movies *Cabaret* and *All That Jazz*. Never before or since has a director been so obsessed with the Dark Side. It became his trademark. And Stephen Sondheim, more concerned with constantly trying new things than with being consciously "dark," forged a parallel path through the years with shows like *West Side Story, Gypsy, Sweeney Todd, Company, Into the Woods*, and *Assassins*. Many of his musicals explored society's ills—gang war, the disintegration of marriage, oppression of the working class, etc.

In 1968, amidst anti-war protests and demonstrations in Washington, *Hair*, the first rock musical, hit Broadway with all the anger, resentment, and disillusionment of the generation of which it was born. It was perhaps the angriest musical ever on Broadway, and its words and music heralded a new age—the age of the realistic and "relevant" musical, which in today's society also meant "Dark." Soon, other rock musicals followed with equally unpleasant themes, including *Pippin, The Rocky Horror Show, Dreamgirls, Little Shop of Horrors,* and others.

In the late 1980s, the "Pop Opera" came into its own—stories told in the structure and epic proportions of grand opera and in the vocabulary of popular music, owing their genesis to the rock operas of Andrew Lloyd Webber and Tim Rice, including *Jesus Christ Superstar* and *Evita.* These shows, *Les Misérables, Phantom of the Opera, Miss Saigon,* and others, with their tragic plots and characters, were the inevitable union of classical opera and the Broadway musical.

It has been fascinating for us during the creation of this show to see how different writers approach that side of us we try to suppress, some using comedy and others tragedy to explore that twilight zone of the human psyche where revenge is just and murder is justified. It gives us a deeper understanding of the human condition and of that uniquely American art form, musical theatre.

That said, we hope you enjoy Dark Side II, dedicated to everyone who loves the musical theatre and, more importantly, to those who think musicals are only silly love songs and sappy happy endings.

Editor's Note: If this is Dark Side 2, *where's* Dark Side 1? *The reason this is* Dark Side 2 *is that the first* Tribute to the Dark Side *was done by many of the same people with CenterStage Theatre Company several years earlier.*

REMEMBERING DARK SIDE 2

Before each performance began, we were to gradually filter onto the stage and sit at tables, cocktail-style, in the "nightclub," and create characters who would chat realistically while the acts would go on. Tracy, Beth, and I were assigned to a table. At one of the first rehearsals, one of us—the memory escapes me as to which one—began a conversation about our fictional boss at the department store. The other two joined in, badmouthing this fictional boss. Throughout the rehearsal process and into performances, we kept these department store worker characters, and the improvised chatter grew more and more detailed until we not only knew our own characters, but we had assembled an outside life at this imaginary job which consisted of another twenty or so people with whom we worked. (Most of them were slackers, of course.) I admit there were times that our work stories became so involved and entertaining that we were slightly disappointed when the songs, the real focus of *Dark Side II*, began. During the show, the cast members all took turns performing songs and placing ourselves as the clientele in this nightclub. After one particular number, Quentin and I were dressed up and were to filter to the tables while Kevin sang "Wanting Things." Each night during this song, Quentin and I created a background tableau. We'd notice each other, make brief eye contact, then make prolonged eye contact, then offer a smile. This little affair built throughout the song, with Quentin making suggestive winks and I dabbing the glow of perspiration from my throat. When the song ended, neither had made a move from our chairs, and I'd leave, with only a backward glance shared to tell what might have been.

—Johanna Schloss, cast member

I always felt really terrible for Michelle Collier when she had to choreograph me. I am the type of actor whose body refuses to cooperate with me when it comes to learning dance moves. This was no exception in *Dark Side 2*. Kevin, Keith, Tracy and I were to perform a Motown-esque song called "Steppin' to the Bad Side" from *Dreamgirls*. Kevin and Keith had rhythm and picked up on the moves pretty readily. Tracy and I, on the other hand, weren't so fortunate. I must say, however, "Steppin' to the Bad Side" turned out to be very cool and a big part of its success was due to the amount of time Michelle spent with us. I appreciate all she did and if you're reading this, Michelle, thank you for not letting me look like a complete idiot!

—Dan Sattel, cast member

Though it was unconscious on my part, I think this show kind of announced to the world what kind of company New Line was going to be, that we were going to be doing musical theatre about sex and drugs and death and every potentially offensive topic ever to headline a newspaper. I was determined to make "Big Spender" true to Bob Fosse's original intentions, to be about carnality, not sexiness, to be lustful and hard and disturbing. I wanted people to sit up and listen, to pay attention like they didn't usually pay attention when they went to a musical. I wanted to say to them, "musicals are not always what you think they are" and prove to them that musical theatre was just as substantial, just as serious, just as powerful, just as muscular as theatre that lacks music. This was just a few months before we would tackle Sondheim's *Assassins* and change New Line and St. Louis audiences forever.

—Scott Miller, director

Breaking Out in Harmony

◆

a world premiere
Book, Music, and Lyrics by Scott Miller
March 18-26, 1994
New City School Theatre, St. Louis

THE CAST
Tucker Goodman—Kent Hobson
Steven Goodman—Kevin Collier
Anne Goodman—Dena O'Malley
Darcy Bowles—Kat Smith
Sherman Bowles—Michael Shreves
Lydia Bowles—Kim Wolterman
Bash Crockett—Dan Sattel
Trish Young—Amy Jayne
Marge Blodgett—Kinsella Berry
Christy Cable
Whitney Furlow
Curtis Singleton

THE ARTISTIC STAFF
Director—Scott Miller
Production Consultant—Sara Lee Hart
Lighting Designer—Steven P. Dohrmann

Stage Manager—Amy Lanning
Set Coordinator—Kevin Collier
Logo Design—Steve Kutheis

THE BAND
Piano—Chris Hegarty
Percussion—Adam Kopff

THE REVIEWS

"There are a lot of truths—and a lot of questions—in *Breaking Out in Harmony*...Miller has dealt with a subject that continues to make news and cause controversy...There are many problems in the New Line Theatre production, but the drama has sufficient backbone to stand upright and deliver its message...Despite the shortcomings, Miller has written a musical that is 'about something,' and about something important too. It's worth seeing, thinking about, and most important, acting on."—Joe Pollack, *St. Louis Post-Dispatch*

"Some of *Breaking Out*'s songs are rousers."—Harry Weber, *The Riverfront Times*

DIRECTOR'S NOTES

In this new musical, three members of the school board of the fictional Harmony, Missouri school district break into their high school library after hours and remove eleven "objectionable" books. Their teenage children find out and launch a protest (one of the kids even figures out how to turn the issue into a profit-making venture), and the controversy divides the community. Despite the students' protests, the board votes officially to keep the books off the shelves, so the students go to the local ACLU for help. The actual case on which the show is based, Pico v. Island Trees, went on for seven years and ended up in the U.S. Supreme Court.

But this is not an isolated case. In fact, since Ronald Reagan took office in 1980, censorship cases have been increasing dramatically every year. Parents continue to demand the removal of everything from Dr. Seuss and Stephen King to the Bible. An organization in Washington, D.C. called People for the American Way tracks the hundreds of challenges to materials in schools each year. Nearly half of the challenges are successful.

But our show isn't only about censorship. The other big issue in *Breaking Out in Harmony* is the question of when a child is old enough to make his own way in the world. The students believe that by age 17 they can make mature decisions for themselves. Yet with the continuing increase of guns and drugs among American teenagers, their parents believe they have good cause to worry about their children and about the many influences on their children's attitudes. Who can honestly say they have nothing to worry about?

Breaking Out in Harmony doesn't try to answer these questions. It merely explores the fears and motivations behind the people on both sides of these very complex issues. In an increasingly dangerous world, parents find it more and more difficult to stop protecting their children. And in the midst of an information explosion, teenagers see so many things they want to explore and discover, and they don't want their parents holding them back. Unfortunately, a case like this one puts the concerns of parents and their children into direct conflict.

The New York Times said about the original case, "The controversy...points directly to fundamental questions about the nature of community in modern American society." One of the judges ruling on the case wrote, "The use of governmental power to condemn a book touches the central nervous system of the first amendment." And the debate rages on today, over everything from Madonna's book, *Sex*, to the author of the Winnie-the-Pooh books.

Thank you for joining us tonight for this roller-coaster ride through the American education system, the American family, and the U.S. Constitution. We hope you enjoy yourselves, and we hope you find lots of things to talk about on the drive home.

REMEMBERING BREAKING OUT IN HARMONY

I'll never forget one performance during *Breaking Out in Harmony*. One of the leading women was very difficult to work with, and one night, an hour before a performance, she showed up with her parents and demanded free tickets for them. Now, we never gave actors free tickets for family members. But this actress told me that either I give her free tickets or she'd quit the show right then. (Being a small company, we did not have understudies.) I didn't see how I could give her tickets without giving all the other actors tickets, which would kill our ticket sales. So I stood my ground and refused. She stormed out of the theatre screaming at me that she quit. The cast went crazy. Would she come back? Was she really quitting? I calmly assured everyone that she would be back, secretly terrified that she would not. Finally, she returned to the dressing room about four minutes before curtain and put on her make-up and costume quickly without saying a word to anyone. She did the show and finished the run, though she never said another word to me. Since that incident, I've become very attuned to "attitude," and if an actor shows even the hint of attitude in auditions, I won't even consider them. I don't ever need to go through that again.

—Scott Miller, author and director

Breaking Out in Harmony taught me a really big, important lesson about writing—that conclusions belong in the audience. Good theatre never tells an audience what to think. It presents a story, issues, questions, and then asks the audience to think about it and come up with their own answers and draw their own conclusions. But in *Harmony* I told the audience exactly what I thought they were supposed to think in the finale, and though the finale was a pretty good song, it emasculated the show. I was starting to feel good about myself as a writer and without realizing it, I got really pretentious and self-righteous. It hurt the show. But I learned my lesson. I hope.

—Scott Miller, author and director

Assassins

Music and Lyrics by Stephen Sondheim
Book by John Weidman
June 17-25, 1994
St. Marcus Theatre, St. Louis

THE CAST
The Balladeer/Lee Harvey Oswald—Dan Carter
John Wilkes Booth—Anthony Mullin
Charles Guiteau—Gary Cox
Leon Czolgosz—Kevin Collier
Giuseppe Zangara—Dan Sattel
Samuel Byck—Joe Blackerby
Sara Jane Moore—Amy Jayne
Lynette "Squeaky" Fromme—Johanna Schloss
John Hinckley—Andrew Nowak
The Proprietor—Leo Schloss
Emma Goldman—Laura Beard Aeling
Michelle Laflen
Andy Wolterman

THE ARTISTIC STAFF
Directors—Scott Miller and Steve Kutheis
Music Director—Scott Miller

Set and Props Coordinator—Greg Hunsaker
Lighting Designer—Steven P. Dohrmann
Sound Designer—Greg Rosebrock
Graphic Designer—Tracy Collins

THE BAND
Piano—Debbie Bernardoni
Keyboards—Scott Miller
Percussion—Luis Fernández

THE REVIEWS

"A surprisingly effective theater piece, in spite of, or perhaps because of, its unusual subject matter. The current production by the New Line Theatre brings out the best the show has to offer…The disparate elements of the show come together in large part because of the teamwork of the New Line cast. Individually, the performers all have fine moments, but they are at their best in what they do together."—Gerry Kowarsky, *St. Louis Post-Dispatch*

"New Line Theatre's current production at the St. Marcus Theatre shores up the unity of this analysis of presidential assassins…*Assassins* is ambitious, fascinating work."—Bob Wilcox, *The Riverfront Times*

"Anyone who tackles *any* Sondheim show and succeeds in entertaining without embarrassing themselves is a worthy force. But this group seems to go beyond that and strives for perfection in every aspect."—Steve Allen, KFUO-FM

DIRECTOR'S NOTES

Assassins is a musical character study of the men and women who have tried to kill U.S. presidents, and of the reasons, obsessions, and protests that led each of them to this extreme act. Some did it for political reasons, others for personal reasons, others still because they were genuinely crazy.

The show's creators don't ask you to sympathize with the assassins, only to spend some time with them and realize that they are real and complicated people—much more than faceless "assassins." They are as much a product of their times and of our American society as any one of us. When we wonder why kids are killing each other on our streets, we would do well to listen to these nine Americans. Their feelings of impotence, powerlessness, and unfulfilled dreams are the feelings so many of us experience today. The message that any one of us could become one of the characters onstage is unsettling but truer than we might want to believe.

This is an unusual musical not just because of its subject matter, but also because of its structure. In many ways, it's more a revue than a traditional musical, a revue of songs and scenes ricocheting back and forth through American history. Some are outrageously funny, some frightening, some deeply moving; like America, *Assassins* is a melting pot.

Strolling through it all is a Balladeer, the personification of the stories, myths, and songs that we pass down generation to generation. Composer Stephen Sondheim and playwright John Weidman propose that many of these assassins were inspired by the stories of those who went before them. To dramatize this, John Wilkes Booth actually suggests to Zangara in 1933 and Oswald in 1963 that they kill the president. The shooting gallery proprietor who sells guns to the assassins in the opening scene perhaps represents a country where easy access to guns and a too-hyped American Dream makes these nine people see only one alternative to their problems.

Booth and the other assassins sing, "Everybody's got the right to be happy." They believe that their guaranteed right to the pursuit of happiness also guarantees them the right to attain that happiness—which is something altogether different. When the mythic American Dream eludes them, they feel cheated, ignored, stepped on.

Earl Warren said, "The only thing we learn from history is that we do not learn." We'd like to think that isn't true. We think that by understanding these nine people, we may be better equipped to help others like them—before they become killers.

So enjoy the show, and when the assassins ask you in the song, "Another National Anthem," to join them, imagine just for a moment the fame, the attention, the chance to change the world. And then be thankful that the pressures of our modern world haven't pushed you to that extreme.

Yet.

REMEMBERING ASSASSINS

Anthony Mullins took on the role of John Wilkes Booth in the original New Line production of *Assassins*. Anthony is a gentleman of English descent and his accent still reflects his heritage, although he was attempting to affect a southern drawl. During early rehearsals, it's important to develop a bond with your cast mates, some commonality that you can share. In the case of the cast of *Assassins*, the first common thing discovered was a good sense of humor. Anthony was rehearsing a very intense scene in which his vocal tone and pitch were quite fevered. Anthony himself was quite fevered toward the end of the production (but that's another story—he did go on, as he himself was wont to say). In any case the balance of the cast sat in the house watching and listening. Anthony, in an impassioned moment and in his best "southern" accent, exclaimed, "It shahns so braht, yoo got ta shae yo ahss!" There was silence in the house. Then exchanged looks. Then, one of the cast in the house said, "Did he just say 'it shines so bright you've got to shave your ass?'" "Everyone exploded in laughter. Later, it was discovered that the line was, "It shines so bright, you've got to shade your eyes."

—Leo Schloss, "Proprietor"

One of the more colorful members of the cast was Michelle Laflen. *Assassins* is a very intense show, and as opening night approached, the cast was concerned about their ability to impart the deep emotional intricacies to the audience. Luckily, Michelle's boyfriend Kenny started coming to rehearsals about a week before the show opened. You see, when you've been through a script fifty times, it's difficult to judge its impact. Having a new person experience the production always brings a fresh perspective. Well, almost always. One night, at the conclusion of the rehearsal and the subsequent (and generally lengthy) notes, I hopped down off the stage and began to look for my things to gather before leaving: car keys, jacket, script. My script was missing. I said, "Hey, does anybody know where my script is?" Michelle responded, "Oh Kenny has it. I think he's in the bathroom." I said, "He can keep it." But I digress. As the cast gathered in the green room before the final dress rehearsal, Michelle spoke up: "Hey, everybody. I just wanted to let you know the show is really great. Kenny said so. He's never emotional, but last night he got choked up watching rehearsal." Oh great. We know we're a success gang—Kenny wept.

—Leo Schloss, "Proprietor"

During the Copland-esque singing of "Big Bill," Kevin Collier as Leon Czolgosz waited in line to meet President William McKinley at the Great Pan-American Exposition in Buffalo. The line of folks (Leo, Michele, Laura, and that one boy) extended downstage from the invisible President upstage to Czolgosz, who was waiting not to shake the President's hand, but to assassinate him. Tech week came, and Kevin and the other gun-totin' assassins were given starter pistols to use. They created a pretty good bang when they went off. For the McKinley assassination, Kevin and his gun were to make it to the head of the line for the climax of the song when Czolgosz, on an abrupt musical caesura, would shoot the President. But it never failed—or rather, it always did. During every dress/tech, Kevin moved to the head of the line, aimed the gun towards the audience (where the invisible McKinley stood), and pulled the trigger. Nothing. The first couple times were funny. But when it happened repeatedly—the gun working perfectly before the rehearsal, then not working at such a crucial moment—well, let's just say Kevin's goddammits and other choice expletives became more and more explosive. And from the point of view of the success of the moment in the show, it certainly made all of us nervous. However, most of us stifled peals of laughter when we considered the possibility of rewriting the show—and American history—so that Leon Czolgosz, instead of assassinating William McKinley, just looked at him, real mean-like, and gave him a good cussin' out.

—Johanna Schloss, "Squeaky"

The first time I directed *Assassins* was the greatest thrill of my life. It was the first time I had directed a show that was truly a masterpiece, the first time I really submerged myself fully into a show, lived it, slept it, thought about nothing else. We had a very talented cast and it turned out so well. Even my mother, who I expected to hate it, found it compelling and mesmerizing. It was the first step in her conversion to the person who now prefers *Floyd Collins* and *The Cradle Will Rock* to *Brigadoon* and *Hello, Dolly*.

Assassins is the bravest show ever written, a masterpiece of subtlety, of characterization, of confrontation, of psychology, of pure, brazen theatricality. It was terribly disturbing to watch and it unnerved each audience through its stubborn refusal to judge these assassins, to take the easy, safe road. It let each assassin speak for him-or herself. Some of them were clearly crazy, but some of them were clearly *not*—and that was the most disturbing thing of all. The message of *Assassins* is that the people who try to kill presidents are more like you and me than we'd like to believe. It's a message most people don't want to hear, but it's one everyone should hear. Ultimately it thrilled audiences every night and was New Line's first genuine triumph, as if our little company had finally grown to full maturity. It was a turning point for New Line and for me, both artistically and personally.

The other reason *Assassins* was special to me, personally, is that early in the rehearsal process, my position at my "real job" was eliminated and I found myself unemployed for the first time in my life. My search for a new job was admittedly half-hearted because I discovered the incredible joy of dedicating my time fully to a show. No more did my job get in the way. No more did I have to work on the show only *after* work. Now it *was* my work. This was when I realized I was meant to be a freelancer. And I haven't had a traditional desk job since then.

One more note. I honestly believe that every high school in America should be forced to produce *Assassins* every four years. With gun violence in our schools reaching epidemic proportions, we must try to understand *why* people get angry, *why* they feel left out by the American Dream, *why* a gun makes them feel empowered—all issues addressed eloquently and intelligently by *Assassins*. This is the one show that could start a dialogue that might lead us to some real answers.

—Scott Miller, director

Pippin

◆

Music and Lyrics by Stephen Schwartz
Book by Roger O. Hirson
October 28-November 5, 1994
St. Marcus Theatre, St. Louis

THE CAST

Pippin—Dan Sattel
Leading Player—Amy Jayne
Charles/Berthe—Kevin Collier
Fastrada—Laura Beard Aeling
Lewis—Leo Schloss
Catherine—Lisa Karpowicz
The Sweet Faced Player—Beck Hunter
The Player with Fire—Jason "Skippy" Kastrup
The Manly Player—Matthew R. Kerns

THE ARTISTIC STAFF

Director—Scott Miller
Choreographer—Michelle Collier
Production Consultant—Sara Lee Hart
Lighting Designer—Kathleen Mayhew
Assistant Lighting Designer—Renee Sevier
Set Coordinator—Greg Hunsaker

Lighting Technician—Kim Wood
Graphic Design—Tracy Collins

THE BAND
Piano—Debbie Bernardoni
Keyboards—Thomas Reed
Percussion—Adam Kopff

THE REVIEWS

"If you like musical theatre that goes for the guts, head for the St. Marcus Theatre…where New Line's *Pippin* runs."—Bob Wilcox, *The Riverfront Times*

"*Pippin* seems to me to be New Line's slickest production to date—skilled cast, excellent technical work, and polished vision…The pit band is nothing short of outstanding."—Harry Weber, *The Riverfront Times*

DIRECTOR'S NOTES

Stephen Schwartz and Roger Hirson created a pleasant little musical called *The Adventures of Pippin* in the early 1970s. But after director Bob Fosse was through re-writing it, it was a cynical, sexual, slickly decadent morality play. When Schwartz raised too many objections to Fosse's changes, he was banned from rehearsals. But after it closed on Broadway, Schwartz had his ideas restored to the script and many of Fosse's changes taken back out, for future productions. New Line's production returns to Fosse's original dark vision of Pippin's quest for fulfillment and identity.

Pippin is a young man with no idea what he wants from his life. Luckily, a traveling troupe of players appears who have helped other young men in Pippin's predicament. They offer to play out his life for him—with colored lights, music and dance, comedy and drama—so that he can try things in his search for fulfillment. With the players' help, his quest becomes a roller coaster ride of razzle-dazzle entertainment and seductively dangerous excesses.

What Pippin doesn't realize though, is that the players' only goal is for him to do their Grand Finale. They make sure he fails at everything so that the finale will be his only remaining opportunity to find perfection. But it's not until the big moment arrives that they tell Pippin what he has to do. They want him to get in a box and set himself on fire—"a glorious synthesis of life and death, and life again!" They want him to commit suicide, live on stage.

When Pippin resists, the Leading Player offers the opportunity to the audience. We can do the finale instead of Pippin. She says to us, "If you should decide to do so, we'll be there for you, waiting. Why, we're right inside your heads."

Up until that point, Pippin is a morality tale with the unpleasant lesson that complete fulfillment doesn't exist. Like John Hinckley and Lee Harvey Oswald in last season's *Assassins*, Pippin thinks the world owes him happiness. When he can't find it, he's angry, confused, bitter. He's told he has to settle for an average life and the fulfillment of none of his ideals.

But when Leading Player says to us, "Why, we're right inside your heads," suddenly it's a whole new ballgame. The players are in Pippin's mind. In fact, the whole show is Pippin's fever dream, a hallucination full of the magic he never found in his life, all happening in the moment before he kills himself. His family is populated by perverse stereotypes, his fantasies filled with frightening characters of his own creation. In reality, Pippin has been causing himself to fail at everything throughout the show, and he has been convincing himself to commit suicide.

We wonder why murder and suicide among teenagers continues to increase. Maybe Pippin knows why. We create outrageous expectations for our young people and then sabotage their chances at attaining them, asking them to grow up faster with each generation. We rarely offer them role models and we destroy the ones they have, people like O.J.

Simpson, Michael Jackson, Clarence Thomas, even Captain Kirk. We tell them they can have anything they want, but it's not true. As rock star Kurt Cobain discovered recently, when everything else is trashed, all that's left is the Grand Finale.

REMEMBERING PIPPIN

If you know Scott, you know of his insistence that his actors go "over the top" in their performances. I never really had a problem with that notion until I did *Pippin*. Scott wanted me to play Pippin like a spoiled-rotten, annoying kid. I would like to repeat loud and clear for those of you that saw *Pippin*—SCOTT MADE ME DO IT! I have never really fought Scott on any of his directorial decisions, but this one drove me crazy. No matter what I did, it wasn't big enough or wasn't "animated" enough. To add fuel to the fire, I had been suckered by Leo Schloss and Scott to quit smoking during the length of our rehearsal schedule and performances, so my voice had a fighting chance at hitting the demanding vocal part. (Side note: I said "suckered" because Leo promised to quit as well so I wouldn't be going through hell alone, and I later found out that he hadn't and both of them had been lying to me the whole time. I've since forgiven them for this horrible deceit). Anyway, I was a little edgy and Scott kept telling me to "go bigger, go bigger." It was frustrating to say the least. Finally, I said to myself, "He's never going to let up until you look like a complete idiot." With this new realization, I transformed Pippin into the most annoying, self-absorbed human being I could imagine…and Scott loved it. You want to get on Scott's good side? Annoy the heck out of him.—Dan Sattel, "Pippin"

Laura Beard Aeling is quite the bohemian. She's a performing artist. She's a visual artist. She's a creative talent. At the time we were doing *Pippin*, she worked for a company that made large, blow-up, three-dimensional versions of Edvard Munch's famous painting *The Scream*. On the first night, the cast gathered for the initial read-through of the script for *Pippin*. In addition to the older, crustier veterans of New Line, there were new faces. Matt Kearns, Skippy Kastrup, and Beck Hunter were the young kids of the crowd. Fresh-faced. Impressionable. Wide-eyed. The cast was asked to take turns in sharing their names and something about themselves with everyone. Laura announced that this was her second New Line production and that, "I make designer inflatables." The three young cast members glanced curiously at each other and then at me. As Laura continued, I said to the rookies, "Sans orifice." Laura, without taking a breath and in the middle of her sentence turned to me and said, "Philistine," and went right on with her introduction.

—Leo Schloss, "Lewis"

I wanted to do *Pippin* to shut up all the people who were always telling me what a silly, shallow piece of irrelevance it is. I think it's one of the best of the American musicals, and not just because of Bob Fosse's original choreography. The more I worked on this show, the more I understood that this is not a show about Charlemagne's son; it's a show about a spoiled, aimless college grad trying to find himself in the morally and emotionally barren landscape of modern-day America. Only from that perspective does everything in it make sense. And my other revelation—that the entire show must be happening in Pippin's head, that in fact he is his own tormentor—seems to be the only way this show works. Yet I've never seen anybody else do it that way. Because the original was full of razzle-dazzle, people missed all the red meat in it. It really does work when you let it, when you respect it. *Pippin* is a rich, complicated, smart piece of theatre about a very real, very flawed central character that addresses some extremely important issues in American life. And I've realized, after doing *Pippin* and other overly maligned shows, that most of the time when people blame their mediocre productions on mediocre material, it's almost always the production's fault and not the material's. I have found again and again, with *Pippin, Anyone Can Whistle, Assassins, Passion, Songs for a New*

World, and *Floyd Collins*—all shows that have been heavily criticized—that if you give a show your greatest effort, your greatest and deepest thought, and if you always assume a problem is yours and not the show's, the show will often reveal itself to be the masterpiece only the fanatics knew it was.—Scott Miller, director

One of my favorite memories of *Pippin* was due to one of the disadvantages of the St. Marcus Theatre. Because the theatre was in a church basement, the ceiling was fairly low, and because the stage was raised two feet, it was only nine feet from the stage floor to the ceiling. Adding to that, Kevin Collier, who played Charlemagne, was six-foot-eight. So poor Kevin had to really watch for any lights hanging above the stage. In one extended musical scene, "Spread a Little Sunshine," Kevin had to enter and exit the stage several times. In rehearsals, each time he'd enter, he'd walk onstage and—*bam!*—slam his forehead right into one of the lights. It happened every night, every entrance during this scene. The first time we were worried if he was hurt; every time after that we'd all giggle like third graders. It was just such a ridiculous sight. (I'm not sure why we never thought about moving the light.) Somehow, he finally learned to avoid it and I don't think he ever hit that light during a performance.—Scott Miller, director

In the Blood

◆

a world premiere
Book, Music, and Lyrics by Scott Miller
May 5-20, 1995
St. Marcus Theatre, St. Louis

THE CAST
Zachary Church—Jim Freund
Adam Graham—Leo Schloss
Rebecca Young—Laura Beard Aeling
Chaz Williams—Andrew Nowak
Danny Hooper—Keith Price
Ruby—Lisa Garcia Fensterman
Jeannie—Johanna Schloss
J.D.—Scott A. Trip
Ricki—Victoria Edrington

THE ARTISTIC STAFF
Director—Scott Miller
Lighting Designer—Steven P. Dohrmann
Set Coordinator—Greg Hunsaker
Graphic Designer—Tracy Collins

THE BAND
Piano—Debbie Bernardoni
Percussion—Adam Kopff

THE REVIEWS

"Ideas loom large in this work. The central one is ingenious…Two things do work for me in *In the Blood*. One—and it surprised me—was the vampire business…The other thing is the love story between the vampire and the hematologist…Much of that emotional conviction grows from Miller's music, which is, I think, the best score he's done for a show."—Bob Wilcox, *The Riverfront Times*

"The dialogue has the ring of situation comedies with characters exchanging glib one-liners and bantering about relationships in clichés. Conflicts lead to high-voltage confrontations, but the verbal fireworks do not result in a choice or a resolution."—Gerry Kowarsky, *St. Louis Post-Dispatch*

AUTHOR'S NOTES

I've come a long way since the first musical I wrote back in 1981. Since then, I've written traditional book musicals (shows with a linear plot line), concept musicals, an absurdist musical comedy, a political musical, even an educational musical about the history of astronomy (no kidding).

This was the first time I've ever had a public reading and discussion of one of my shows, and it was a wonderful experience for me, for the actors, and for the audience. A big crowd showed up at our reading in February—a lot more than we expected—and their comments during the discussion afterward were for the most part intelligent and very useful. Since the reading, I've done a lot of rewriting, cutting, adding, and rearranging to strengthen the show. It's been through four versions so far, the latest of which is still being revised as I write this.

For the first time, I've constructed a score in which musical themes are used to connect characters and dramatic events. For instance, the melody to the chorus of Adam's song "The River of Life" is also the melody to the bridge in Zach's "Hell," in order to connect these two characters emotionally; and it shows up again in their Act II duet, "Alone." A number of other musical themes are sprinkled throughout the evening to link dramatic events and reinforce important concepts (death, loneliness, etc). Most of Stephen Sondheim's scores, Andrew Lloyd Webber's earlier works, shows like *Les Misérables*, and a lot of operas use musical themes in this way, and it's been fascinating playing with these musical puzzle pieces to help tell this story, even if it's only on a subliminal level.

I read a great quote recently, that premises belong on stage, and conclusions belong in the house. In other words, a playwright shouldn't tell his audience what to think; he should present interesting issues and ideas and let them form their own opinions. Of course, this is easier said than done, and it is asking more of an audience than the average musical theatre audience expects. But I have found that New Line's audiences enjoy a challenging theatre piece. As with most of our shows, *In the Blood* addresses a variety of issues. I hope you find it interesting and thought-provoking, as well as a lot of fun.

REMEMBERING IN THE BLOOD

Unintentional pauses onstage are the scariest thing an actor can encounter, and *In the Blood* had a classic. It was one of the last performances, the beginning of the last scene. Leo is onstage, "unconscious" in a hospital bed. Laura is standing next to the bed, but she's losing her voice, and she's blown it out during the performances so that she can now barely make a peep. Andy and Keith are also onstage, all of them waiting for Jim to enter. But Jim is offstage trying to make a costume change and he can't open the fastener on his tux pants to take them off. So there they stand onstage, no one saying a thing as the audience hears the frantic jingling of Jim's belt offstage. Neither Andy nor Keith can think of a single thing to say. There is more than a minute of dead silence—an eternity onstage. Finally Jim yells his first line from offstage. No one responds. He keeps jingling. After what seems like ten minutes but is actually only about two minutes, Jim finally makes it onstage, just in time to keep me from having a coronary embolism at the piano. After the show, we all have a good stiff drink and I tell Jim he can leave the tux pants on for the last scene.

—Scott Miller, author/director

Company

Music and Lyrics by Stephen Sondheim
Book by George Furth
November 10-18, 1995
St. Marcus Theatre, St. Louis

THE CAST

Robert—Michael Davidson
Harry—Gary Cox
Sarah—Lisa Karpowicz
Peter—Joseph Taro
Susan—Johanna Schloss
David—Greg Hunsaker
Jenny—Sherry Frank
Paul—Andrew Nowak
Amy—Laura Beard Aeling
Larry—Keith Price
Joanne—Teresa Doggett
Marta—Angela Shultz
April—Michelle Collier
Kathy—Heather Holland

THE ARTISTIC STAFF
Director—Scott Miller
Choreographer—Michelle Collier
Lighting Designer—Kathy Mayhew
Assistant Lighting Designer—Renee Sevier
Set Designers—Greg Hunsaker, Laura Beard Aeling
Scenic Painter—Andy Milner
Graphic Designer—Tracy Collins

THE BAND
Piano—Catherine Edwards
Percussion—Adam Kopff

THE REVIEWS

"In *Company*, Stephen Sondheim wrote a lovely song called "Sorry/Grateful" about the ambiguities of marriage. New Line Theatre's presentation of the musical misses that subtle touch. It is unambiguously sorry."—Judith Newmark, *St. Louis Post-Dispatch*

"Perhaps giving the audience too much to notice and think about can be dangerous."—Susan Wells, *West End Word*

DIRECTOR'S NOTES

It has been said that you can do anything you want in a musical as long as you do it within the first ten minutes. In other words, audiences will accept any style of music, any unusual structural devices, as long as the show's particular ground rules are established in the first ten minutes of the show. And that's exactly what the first song in *Company* does. The opening bars of the song "Company" instantly establish the frenetic, pulsing rhythm of the city and of modern life. When the voices enter, the couples are established as the focus of the show, along with their smothering affection for Robert. We realize that everything we see will be through Robert's eyes; and the show's surreal style suggests that it's all happening in Robert's mind, in his memory, as he tries to sort out his questions about commitment.

The couples begin the opening song with their various nicknames for Robert, which will return as a leitmotif (a musical theme representing a particular idea) throughout the score. This quickly segues into short phrases that illustrate how hard it is to communicate with Robert. We hear the voices through Robert's ears, overlapping, overwhelming, smothering. In the last sentence of the song, the title of the show is equated with love, and by implication, both are equated with marriage. Before the song is over, Sondheim has established the style, structure, and pace of the show, the brittle cleverness of the lyrics, important relationships, and the major themes of the show.

Like many of Sondheim's scores, *Company* is filled with commentary songs. In more traditional musicals, songs grow naturally out of dialogue, and characters aren't aware of the fact that they're singing. But in many of the songs in *Company* (and in *Follies, Into the Woods, Assassins,* etc.), the characters step out of the scene and address the audience directly. This makes the audience step back and think about what's happening rather than just feeling. *Company*'s score is also unusual in its extensive use of musical motifs to connect characters and events. The "Bobby Buby" motif used throughout the show focuses our attention on the married couples in opposition to Robert, their attitudes toward him, etc. Both "Tick Tock" (the instrumental piece while Robert and April have sex) and "Being Alive" make interesting use of motifs from many other songs in the show. "Tick Tock" even quotes *The Twilight Zone* theme.

Company is a fascinating musical that uses music as an integral part of the narrative process, while it completely discards the traditional look of chronological storytelling. But very few other musicals have followed its lead. Most later "concept" musicals copied *Company*'s construction but were afraid to totally ignore the conventions of narrative theatre. *Company* stands as one of the greatest innovations in the history of musical theatre, and we can only ask twenty-five years later, isn't it time for someone to take us the next step?

REMEMBERING COMPANY

Everything I needed to know about musicals I learned doing *Company*. Well, while that may not be entirely accurate, I will say that the experience was invaluable in many ways. After dropping out of college, I moved home—completely lost about what to do with my life. I saw the audition notice for *Company*, and must have talked myself in and out of auditioning nearly a hundred times. I was dying to do a Sondheim show (I didn't know people actually produced anything of his besides *Into the Woods*), so I finally resolved myself to going. When I first rehearsed with the cast, I knew I was a part of something incredible. I learned how truly great musicals are constructed. I learned to take chances. I learned what the bond of theatre lovers is like. I took these things, and in time gained the direction and focus I had been seeking.

—Angie Shultz, "Marta"

Out on Broadway

◆

a world premiere
Featuring songs from *Bye Bye Birdie, Girl Crazy, She Loves Me, Dear World, Falsettos, Once Upon a Mattress, Merrily We Roll Along, City of Angels, Les Misérables, Kiss of the Spider Woman, Victor/Victoria, Mame, Dreamgirls, Follies, Company, The Robber Bridegroom, Phantom of the Opera, La Cage aux Folles, Passion, Into the Woods, The Secret Garden, The Rothschilds, South Pacific, Assassins,* and other shows
Conceived by Scott Miller
March 1-9, 1996
Additional Performances August 16-24, 1996
St. Marcus Theatre, St. Louis

THE CAST
Chris Brenner, Tracy Collins, Quenten Schumacher II, Keith Thompson, Eddie Webb

THE ARTISTIC STAFF
Director—Scott Miller
Additional Staging—J.T. Ricroft
Lighting Designer—Linda Lawson
Graphic Design—Tracy Collins
Pianist—Scott Miller

THE REVIEWS

"A sweetly rewarding and happy surprise...Not since Tom Clear and Joan Lipkin's *Some of My Best Friends Are* held court has a musical evening so expertly fused the intimacy, politics, and spirit of the St. Marcus...United in song and spirit, the cast and audience celebrate the fusion of a Broadway past into the home for a community's political future."—Mike Isaacson, *The Riverfront Times*

"Entertaining and thought-provoking, *Out on Broadway*, the new revue from New Line Theatre, offers musical theatre with a decidedly different twist...It's what theater, at its best, is for."—Judith Newmark, *St. Louis Post-Dispatch*

"A most thought-provoking, touching, and entertaining production."—*News-Telegraph*

"Some of the evening's best moments owe their power to flawless harmonizing."—Harry Weber, *The Riverfront Times*

DIRECTOR'S NOTES
(March 1996)

Gay men and lesbians have been playing straight characters since time began. They've had to sing about a kind of love they never felt, never able (until recently) to sing about the feelings they actually have. Stars like Danny Kaye, Larry Kert, George Rose, Jack Cassidy and many others never had a chance to explore in their work the issues they faced in their daily lives.

Gay or bisexual writers, including Stephen Sondheim, Cole Porter, Jerry Herman, Leonard Bernstein, Noel Coward, Lorenz Hart, Arthur Laurents, Howard Ashman, and so many others have had to "transpose" their feelings in order to write for the characters in their shows.

Only a few gay musicals have ever played on Broadway. And though TV and movies are finally accepting gay characters as something more than a punch line, the Broadway musical is much slower to do the same. However, in regional theatres gay issues are being explored in many new musicals by writers like Mark Savage, Linda Eisenstein, Chris Jackson, myself, and others. Two songs from Mark Savage's new musical, *The Ballad of Little Mikey* will be performed tonight. This spring, an album of songs from gay musicals will be released by AEI Records, including songs from *The Ballad of Little Mikey* and the gay vampire musical *In the Blood*, which New Line premiered last season.

So tonight we present the history of Broadway musicals the way it should have been.

Every song you'll hear tonight was chosen for a reason. "You Have to Be Carefully Taught" was written about racism, but its message against intolerance is as relevant today as ever, as religious extremists demonize gays and lesbians. "In My Own Lifetime" and "Do You Hear the People Sing" are particularly potent, reminding us of the all the work we have to do. "Children Will Listen" is a warning to those political and religious leaders who would promote prejudice and fear instead of understanding. And in this explosive election year, "Our Time" and "Everybody's Got the Right" are no longer just show tunes—they are battle cries.

"Everything Possible" is the song we all wish someone had sung to us when we were little, a song that we hope will be sung to children from now on.

Very few of these songs were written in the context in which you find them tonight, but I think you'll be surprised at how easily they work this way. The experiences we're exploring tonight are universal. A love song written for a straight couple fits a gay couple no less perfectly: One lyric sums it all up: "They're writing songs of love, but not for me..." Well, tonight these songs are for us all.

DIRECTOR'S NOTES
(August 1996)

Well, here we are, back "Out" at the St. Marcus.

This is the first time New Line has ever done a show a second time. It's the first time we thought a piece was important enough. We decided that if we can reach people this time that we didn't reach the first time, then it's worth doing again.

We didn't realize this show was as special as it is until we put it in front of an audience last March. It's the only gay revue I'm aware of that doesn't make fun of gays and also doesn't ask for pity for gays. It's a very proud, brave, and occasionally political look at being gay in America. This is a show that sees gays as regular people, with the same kind of joy and heartache as everyone else, despite their often unique societal obstacles. And I think that's a big part of what made it so incredibly popular the first time around.

Gay men and lesbians have been playing straight characters since theatre began. We've had to sing about a kind of love we never felt, never able (until recently) to sing about the feelings we actually have. Stars like Danny Kaye, Larry Kert, George Rose, Jack Cassidy, and many others never had a chance to explore in their work the issues they faced in their daily lives.

Gay or bisexual writers, including Cole Porter, Jerry Herman, Leonard Bernstein, Noel Coward, Lorenz Hart, Arthur Laurents, Howard Ashman, and so many others never had a chance to explore their lives in their writing.

Only a few gay musicals have ever played on Broadway. And though TV and movies are finally accepting gay characters as something more than a punch line, the Broadway musical is much slower to do the same. However, in regional theatres gay issues are being explored in many new musicals by writers like Mark Savage, Linda Eisenstein, Cindy O'Connor & Larry.Johnson, Chris Jackson, myself, and others. Two songs from Mark Savage's new musical, *The Ballad of Little Mikey* (which New Line will produce in June 1997) will be performed tonight.

We've made some small changes since the last time we were here—a few songs cut, a few added, a few moved. We hope you like the show even better. Very few of these songs were written in the context in which you find them tonight, but I think you'll be surprised at how easily they work this way.

Many of the experiences we're exploring are indeed universal. As Congress passes new (possibly un-Constitutional) laws to exclude gays and lesbians from legal marriage, as Bob Dole and his friends work to prevent us from enjoying other equal rights, as national religious leaders misuse and misquote the Bible to demonize us, this is an important lesson for his all to take with us.

REMEMBERING OUT ON BROADWAY

What wonderful voices and great people to work with, and more talent that intimidated me. There was so much time and effort put into each song, which I think helped us to make the show our own. I could not believe the audiences we got; they loved us. That was a major high. But I wish I could go back and rerecord the CD. Having the knowledge I have now with several vocal master classes under my belt (trust me, my pants still fit snug), I would sing everything very different. How great we are—the only New Line show that made a CD, but we are not the only ones that should have made one.

—Chris Brenner, cast member

I remember how I felt being involved in such a unique production and how the concept of the show excited me. Using songs traditionally meant for women, but putting a new twist to them by using the male voice and form. As a choreographer, it created challenges that were fun to work out, especially with a cast that was so eager to try anything. We were all limitless, since this had not been done before and we had no

expectations or past "female" interpretations to consider. During rehearsals, we had so much fun creating pictures that would allow the audience to experience each song in a new way. It was amazing to watch as each song took on a new meaning, due to the conscious choices each performer made along the way. I cried, I laughed, I smiled, and I traveled the journey with anticipation…it was better than *Cats*! I was grateful that the St. Louis audiences embraced this production. My fear was that it would be received as "a bunch of men singing songs about other men." The sense of community and love, regardless of the sex or sexual disposition, was felt and experienced by all who attended and shared in the production. Whew! They got it. I was honored to be a part of it all.
—John Ricroft, choreographer

Sweeney Todd

◆

Music and Lyrics by Stephen Sondheim
Book by Hugh Wheeler
June 7-22, 1996
St. Marcus Theatre, St. Louis

THE CAST
Sweeney Todd—Mark Stulce
Anthony Hope—Keith Thompson
Beggar Woman—Laura Beard Aeling
Nellie Lovett—Lisa Karpowicz
Johanna Turpin—Sherry Frank
Beadle Bamford—Michael Dewes
Judge Turpin—Steven R. Johnson
Tobias Ragg—Dan Sattel
Adolfo Pirelli—George M. Jones
Bird Seller—David Blake
Mr. Fogg—Jerry Smith
Cindy Duggan
Judy Moebeck

THE ARTISTIC STAFF
Director—Scott Miller
Assistant Director—Matthew R. Kerns

Lighting Designer—L.D. Lawson
Set Coordinator—Greg Hunsaker
Costumes and Props Designer—Quenten Schumacher II
Special Prop Construction—Pat Edmonds
Graphic Design—Tracy Collins

THE BAND
Piano—Catherine Edwards
Keyboards—Jim Ryan
Percussion—Adam Kopff

THE REVIEWS

"Under director Scott Miller, *Sweeney* appears in a completely different light, pared down and bitterly funny…Miller's treatment makes sense and the tiny, peculiarly shaped St. Marcus Theatre is exactly the right setting for it…To be honest, I've seen *Sweeney Todd* before and never liked it. But this production made me consider it from a different perspective; I appreciate that."—Judith Newmark, *St. Louis Post-Dispatch*

"Ultimately, it is the challenges that make *Sweeney Todd*, like so much Sondheim, a stimulating evening in the theatre."—Box Wilcox, *The Riverfront Times*

"I was amazed at how beautifully the show fits in the tiny St. Marcus Theatre…I'm now convinced that is how it is most effective."—Steve Callahan, KDHX-FM

DIRECTOR'S NOTES

Sweeney Todd is one of only two musicals that Stephen Sondheim has initiated himself (the other is *Passion*). Though the massive original production was very effective, Sondheim has said that he intended it to be an intimate chamber musical with few sets. And that may be the way it is the most effective, the most chilling, the most personal. This is not a show intended to leave an audience happy and safe in the knowledge that Good always triumphs over Evil. *Sweeney Todd* is meant to disturb.

Of the many musical motifs used in *Sweeney Todd*, one of the most interesting—and appropriate—is the *dies irae*. This chant melody from the Mass for the Dead has been used for centuries in music about death and dying. It first appears in "The Ballad of Sweeney Todd" as the melody to the chorus ("Swing your razor wide, Sweeney..."). It's also found, upside-down, as the accompaniment to "The Ballad of Sweeney Todd," and used as underscoring throughout the show. This inverted version also becomes the vocal melody to "My Friends." Thus, the *dies irae* connects the opening number describing Sweeney with both his song about why he will kill ("Barber and His Wife") and his song about how he will kill ("My Friends").

This show has several things to say about human nature and about society. The most obvious statement the authors are making is that we all have the capacity for revenge that Sweeney has. In the last song, the chorus sings to us, "Perhaps today you gave a nod to Sweeney Todd," and later, "Sweeney waits in the parlor hall, Sweeney leans on the office wall. No one can help, Nothing can hide you. Isn't that Sweeney there beside you?"

To some extent, they are saying, we all live in the past, we all make mistakes we regret, and we all have revenge in our hearts at one time or another. Perhaps we don't go to the extremes that Sweeney did; but then again, how often are we put in the very extreme circumstances into which Sweeney has been thrust?

Like Sondheim's *Assassins*, *Sweeney Todd* also makes the case that society is to blame—for the unfair class structure, exploitation of the working classes, the abuse of power, a corrupt government and justice system. Like *Assassins*, the black humor in *Sweeney Todd* allows us to distance ourselves from the horror of what's happening, but it also makes us realize how easily we can trivialize murder and brutality. Is "A

Little Priest" all that different from Oliver Stone's film *Natural Born Killers* or Quenten Tarentino's *Pulp Fiction*? As a society, we have grown numb to death; we see it so much on the news, in television shows, in the movies, that it hardly fazes us anymore. Through wars, urban riots, and "ethnic cleansing," killing has become an impersonal act. And perhaps that's one of Sondheim's points—the fact that Sweeney and Mrs. Lovett can joke about the brutal murders they will commit is an indictment of our culture. But remember that they're not the only ones laughing—so are we.

REMEMBERING SWEENEY TODD

Scott blocked the show using the entire theatre as a stage. The cast was often out among the audience. There were two satellite stages, one on the left of the main stage and one on the right. The main stage was used only as Sweeney's barber shop. Scott blocked the opening number with the cast spaced and staggered the width of the theatre on the floor in front of the main stage. During the song there are quite a few one line solos from various cast members. I think the cast enjoyed watching the audience during the opening number as much as the audience enjoyed watching us. As each solo was performed, the audiences' heads would turn in unison toward the sound. First left, then right, then center. It was quite a funny sight. It was almost like they were watching a tennis match or they were a hundred cats looking at the same piece of string being dangled in front of them.

—Steve Johnson, "Judge Turpin"

I'm sure that everyone who has been involved in theatre has one show that will forever stand out as a career highlight. For me, this highlight is New Line's production of *Sweeney Todd*. Mrs. Lovett possesses a delicious sense of humor and that, paired with her obvious character flaws, provided me with a never-ending source of challenges, pleasures, and memories. One of my least favorite memories of this production, however, occurred on opening night. I was always particularly nervous before my first scene which contained the song "Worst Pies in London," a song in which it is *very* easy to become tongue-tied or drop a line. This night, however, it went flawlessly and I was ecstatic. Just off stage I uttered a very quiet but jubilant "*Yes!*" and in doing so missed the two steps leading down and, instead, fell off the side with my ankle twisted underneath me. As soon as I heard that "crunch" sound and felt the sickening pain, I knew it was sprained. I literally crawled back to the dressing room where everyone thought, at first, that I was just playing some kind of joke. I guess it was the tears streaming down my face that convinced them that I was definitely not pretending. We were able to find a roll of duct tape with which I wrapped my ankle and the show went on. I can honestly say that, on that particular night, at least, I had no trouble finding the right motivation for Mrs. Lovett's cry of anguish as Sweeney throws her into the oven!

—Lisa Karpowicz, "Mrs. Lovett"

Every night, several white shirts and barber cloths would get fake blood on them, and someone had to wash them each night after the show to make sure they were blood-free for the next performance. That task fell to me. Let's talk about stress. I'm disabled. It's my first show in six years. It's my fourth musical in twenty-five years. It's my first Sondheim show. It's a New Line show and I'm working with Scott Miller for the first time. The temperature in the theatre is near one hundred degrees each night. Now, let's add to that, I'm crossing state lines, from Missouri to Illinois, every night with a trunk full of "blood-soaked" clothes. If the police had ever stopped me during that time, they would still be digging up my yard looking for bodies. And yet, New Line's *Sweeney Todd* was the best thing to happen to me in years. It was interesting and a great deal of fun.

—Steve Johnson, "Judge Turpin"

Passion

◆

a St. Louis premiere
Music and Lyrics by Stephen Sondheim
Book by James Lapine
November 15-23, 1996
St. Marcus Theatre, St. Louis

THE CAST

Clara—Deborah Sharn
Captain Giorgio Bachetti—Jim Merlo
Fosca—Laura Beard Aeling
Lieutenant Torasso—J.T. Ricroft
Colonel Ricci—Brett Kristofferson
Doctor Tambourri—Steven R. Johnson
Sergeant Lombardi—Jonathan Stone
Lieutenant Barri—Kevin Collier
Major Rizzoli—Keith Thompson
Private Augenti—Derek Silkebaken
Fosca's Mother—Judy Moebeck
Fosca's Father—Kevin Collier
Count Ludovic—Quenten Schumacher II
The Count's Mistress—Sherry Frank

THE ARTISTIC STAFF
Director—Scott Miller
Assistant Director—Brian Tibbets
Set Designers—Leif Gantvoort and L.D. Lawson
Lighting Designer—Makeesha Coleman
Costume Designer—Quenten Schumacher II
Graphic Design—Tracy Collins

THE BAND
Piano—Debbie Bernardoni
Trumpet—Paul Hecht
Flute/Clarinet—Mark Strathman
Percussion—Adam Kopff

THE REVIEWS

"The New Line Theatre production of *Passion* is a triumph for director Scott Miller and his company…Miller's cast and crew supply the fervor and understanding required to bring out the haunting melancholy of [James] Lapine's book and [Stephen] Sondheim's words and music."—Gerry Kowarsky, *St. Louis Post-Dispatch*

"At once outrageous and courageous, Scott Miller's production…has the audacity and insight to strip away the layers of pretension and seriousness that enveloped the original New York production…resulting in a wild, bold ride for the audience. Bring a friend, because you'll have a lot to talk about…All involved deserve praise for attacking the difficult assignment with considerable intelligence, honesty, and of course, passion."—Mike Isaacson, *The Riverfront Time*

DIRECTOR'S NOTES

At the beginning of *Passion*, Giorgio and Clara sing:
> *Just another love story,*
> *That's what they would claim.*

Another simple love story—
Aren't all of them the same?
No, but this is more...

And they're not just referring to themselves. They're also describing the musical *Passion* itself. It is a love story after all, but it's definitely not like all the rest.

Passion is a tale of deeply felt unconditional love in a world obsessed with physical beauty. It's a profoundly emotional, disturbing story that makes us think about serious issues of love, beauty, passion, and gender roles, even as our hearts break along with Fosca, Giorgio, and Clara.

We were all anxious to work on this show because it's so unlike any other work of the musical theatre. Even for Stephen Sondheim, the greatest rule-breaker working in the art form today, this is still an experiment: his first non-ironic love story. This is not a show in which the authors step back and comment wryly on the follies of love. Instead *Passion* charges head first into the pain and disorienting passion of love. There is nothing separating us from Fosca and her extreme expressions of love, nor from the raw sexuality of Giorgio and Clara.

The greatest joy for an actor or director is to find material that is utterly real, that accurately represents the hopelessly confusing, conflicting human condition, and *Passion* is that kind of show. Even the most serious musicals condense characters into clearly defined essences for dramatic purposes. But this is a show whose story works only because the characters are not essences, but are instead fully formed, deeply complex people. None of the decisions and choices made by these people is black and white. None of the characters is wholly good or bad. Everyone populates the gray middle ground of morality, responsibility, loyalty, and self-preservation.

We're all curious to see how you will respond to this show. We think everyone will have a different reaction, that men and women will disagree, that older people and younger people, married and single people, parents and children will disagree. Everyone will bring their own experiences, past loves and losses, past and present obsessions to Fosca, Giorgio, and Clara's story.

We think it will unsettle you a little, but more importantly, move you greatly. Whatever your reaction, we hope you enjoy the show.

REMEMBERING PASSION

What an incredible, unique show. The mostly sold out audiences were absolutely spellbound every performance. I've never seen anything like that before or since. It was a very dark, sometimes disturbing yet beautiful two-hour show with no intermission. Then there were the boots. Most of the men had to wear these rented boots that squeaked with every step. When the men made a scene change, there was rhythmic squeaking. When they tried to cross backstage, there were the squeaks. There was no way to stop the boots from making noise. Watching the actors backstage trying to walk without making noise was like being at a contortionists' convention. Some walked on their toes, others tried walking on their heels, but they all walked as if they were on a tight rope. Nothing worked. It's a good thing the show held the audiences' attention so well; otherwise they would have thought there were "military mice" in the theatre.

—Steve Johnson, "Dr. Tambourri"

The role of Clara in New Line's production of Stephen Sondheim's musical *Passion* was by far the most erotic role I had experienced and I delighted in it. Believe me, I'd had my share of passionate, scantily clad roles in the past. But the sexual intimacy that Clara and Giorgio expressed onstage, a mere three feet from the first row of the audience, not to mention the attractiveness of my costar, Jim Merlo, was a stirring theatrical experience for me. I remember the night I first kissed Jim. We were doing a publicity photo shoot and Scott suggested that I sit on Jim's lap, in my very sheer nightgown. Jim, God love him, was not wearing a shirt, and he was certainly stirring everyone at the rehearsal—he's one of those guys with perfect chest hair placement and the physique to match. What began as an awkward moment of hesitation turned into scintillating, sensual kissing that seemed to last an eternity. Scott practically had to pull us apart. Many a rehearsal I would lose my way in the lyrics and surrender to the passion of the moment. Men and women alike found Jim appealing; many a man said he was living vicariously through me. Tough luck, guys. Needless to say during performances my professionalism always won out and I ended up thinking about breath (catching my breath, that is!) and vocal technique during our songs together. Little did I know that the following March, Jim would play Marvin to my Trina in *March Of The Falsettos* and he'd leave me for a man. Ah, the fickleness of men!

—Deborah Sharn, "Clara"

During the rehearsal process for *Passion*, I was having very serious thoughts about quitting acting altogether. This was my second show in six years. I played Doctor Tambourri, and Scott and I were having trouble trying to figure out the doctor's motivation for doing the things he did in the show. I was also having a great deal of trouble concentrating and learning my lines. I figured I was rusty and that I was getting too old to do shows. It was very frustrating. Then about three weeks before the show opened I discovered the furnace leak in my home. I had no idea carbon monoxide was slowly killing me. I got the furnace fixed. My mind cleared, I learned my lines and Scott and I had some very good conversations about my character that made sense and helped. In the end I didn't quit theatre, although Scott and others keep begging me to.

—Steve Johnson, "Dr. Tambourri"

I don't know if I've ever worked on a more beautiful, more lush, more thrilling score than *Passion*'s. To live in that music for two months was utterly overwhelming and exhilarating. It may well be the most beautiful music anyone has ever written for the stage. And the story of

Passion, again so utterly overwhelming, so disturbing, so shattering, completely absorbed me. It was all I could think about, not only during the process, but for months after we closed. And then there's our cast— a brilliant, dedicated cast that captured perfectly the pain and beauty and obsession and danger of this dark, scary, soulful tale. There was no greater thrill than watching Laura, Deborah, and Jim, and the others tackle this story night after night. From my admittedly biased position, I really believe we went deeper and took more risks than the original production did. And the other thing that made me so proud of this cast is that *Passion* was one of the most difficult scores we'd ever tackled, and they learned it thoroughly, every note, every rest, every entrance. It occurred to me as we worked on it that the Broadway cast had always had a conductor in front of them cuing every entrance, every difficult passage, but the New Line cast did not have that luxury. Because of the physical intimacy of our shows, there is never a conductor between the actors and the audience. Our actors never had any help in knowing when and where to sing. They had to know the score inside and out, every fascinating twist and turn (and there are a lot!). I asked of them something that had not been asked even of the original Broadway cast, and despite the difficulty, they actually sang it more accurately than the Broadway cast. They sang exactly what Sondheim wrote, and in many cases, with greater depth and meaning because they did not take liberties with Sondheim's music. Lots of performers have said that every note of a Sondheim score counts, that there is a reason for every note and every rest. Never has that been truer than with *Passion*, and I will always be exceptionally proud of how true we were to this glorious score

—Scott Miller, director

Jacques Brel is Alive and Well and Living in Paris

◆

Music and Original French Lyrics by Jacques Brel
Conception, English Lyrics and Additional Material by
Eric Blau and Mort Shuman, based on Brel's Commentary
February 21-March 1, 1997
St. Marcus Theatre, St. Louis

THE CAST
Laura Beard Aeling, Kevin Collier, Johanna Schloss, Mark Stulce

THE ARTISTIC STAFF
Directors—Scott Miller and Brian Tibbets
Scene Painter—Andy Milner
Set Decorator—Leif Gantvoort
Lighting Designer—L.D. Lawson
Lighting Technician—Makeesha Coleman
Costume Coordinator—Quenten Schumacher II
Graphic Designer—Tracy Collins

THE BAND
Piano—Scott Miller
Guitar/Mandolin—Mike Bauer
Bass—Terry Kippenberger
Percussion—Adam Kopff

THE REVIEWS

"New Line Theatre...has taken on the challenge and acquits itself with an entertaining and thoughtful production...directors Scott Miller and Brian Tibbets have understood and captured Brel's smoky, bittersweet flavor."—Judith Newmark, *St. Louis Post-Dispatch*

"Jacques Brel himself may have died a few years ago, but his spirit and his unique songs are indeed alive and well and living at the St. Marcus Theatre...The New Line Theatre's current production captures all the potent poetry of Brel, and it is surprisingly fresh and current, despite the sometimes strong political or social content."—Steve Callahan, KDHX-FM

DIRECTOR'S NOTES

More than any other piece written for the musical stage, *Jacques Brel is Alive and Well and Living in Paris* defies description. It is an evening of independent songs (almost one-act musicals), yet it's not a revue. It doesn't have a plot or even an immediately recognizable cast of characters, so it's not really a book musical.

We think it's a one-character musical with a cast of four. Two women and two men all portray one character: Jacques Brel. The words are Brel's, the opinions, insights, and satiric wit are Brel's. The underlying, sometimes nearly hidden optimism is Brel's. The show is more a character study than anything else, but we must ask if it is a character study of just Jacques Brel the man or also of western civilization at the end of the 20th century?

Jacques Brel was born in Belgium in 1929 but moved to Paris to be a singer and songwriter. By the early 1960s, Brel had established a reputation as one of France's greatest writers and interpreters of modern songs. In 1957, the first American recording of Brel's songs was released. In 1961, Elly Stone sang two Brel songs, "Ne me quitte pas" ("Don't

Leave Me") and "La Valse mille temps," ("The Waltz in 1,000 Time") in a strange off-Broadway revue called *O, Oysters!*

Though the show didn't run long, Stone continued to perform these two songs. In 1968, Eric Blau and Mort Shuman created an off-Broadway musical using twenty-five of Brel's songs, called *Jacques Brel is Alive and Well and Living in Paris*, and it ran for 1,847 performances. The show has been revived twice in New York. A film version was released in 1975, which included an appearance by Brel. Since the show first opened, Brel's songs have been recorded by artists as diverse as David Bowie, Judy Collins, and Barry Manilow. Brel died in 1978 at age 49, but they didn't change the title of the show. You'll see why tonight.

Very few of Jacques Brel's songs are simple and straight-forward. He was a poet as much as a songwriter, and the words he writes often cloak a deeper meaning. So many of the songs in the show are not what they appear to be. "I Loved" is about being in love with the symbols of love instead of with a person. "Bachelor's Dance" is about unrealistic expectations. "My Death" is a view of death as inevitable but patient. "Jackie" is a man who hates his life and wishes he could return to the innocence and simplicity of childhood. "The Statue" condemns the false (and dangerous?) romanticizing of war and soldiering. "Brussels" is about denial in the face of danger. "No Love, You're Not Alone," is about how we project our own sorrow onto someone else so that they will "need" us. Every single song is an adventure and a meditation.

You'll never see another show like this one, and we'll never work on another show like this. So we really treasure this experience.

We hope you will, too.

REMEMBERING JACQUES BREL

This was one of my favorite New Line shows. Not only was the material challenging and inspiring, but also the small company was genuinely warm and supportive. Many events during the run were memorable in their own right—Laura slicing her hand open with her umbrella during "Madeleine" (and finishing the last hour and forty-five minutes of the show with her hand wrapped in whatever clean cloth could be found); Mark hiding words to his songs in the doorway to steal a glance when he could; Scott and Brian demonstrating the complicated choreography of "Carousel" as the four of us watched in fascination and horror; Kevin's incredibly poignant rendition of "The Statue" resonating through a silenced house. However, there is one simple memory that sticks with me, too—the memory of Kevin's and Laura's hands holding mine while we stood in semi-darkness at the edge of the stage and sang "The Desperate Ones" and "If We Only Have Love." At the end of each of those songs, there would be a quiet moment, and just before the audience applauded, we'd lightly squeeze each other's hands. That remains one of my favorite theatre moments.

—Johanna Schloss, cast member

One of the most rewarding experiences that I had working with New Line was assisting with the choreography on both "Marathon" and "Carousel" for *Jacques Brel is Alive and Well and Living in Paris*. These two songs provided such a good framing mechanism for the entire show, incorporating all of the show's warnings and prophecies into fiercely overt language and imagery. The choreography for both songs needed to mirror those warnings accurately. This was a large task because of the wildly different types of music in the show. Staying true to the music was necessary, and in the end, it is what made those two songs most effective.

For "Marathon," the lyrics "flashed" different images of various aspects of the twentieth century, ranging from "the twenties roar because there's bathtub gin" to the prophetic "and the nineties whimper and the century hangs." Scott and I spent hours working with different ideas until we finally ended up with a frantic, whirlwind tour of the century, the actors mimicking the lyrics. It opened the evening very nicely and set the stage for the rest of the show.

The choreography for "Carousel" gave us fits because of the repetition and increasingly frantic pace of the music. Again, the music dictated the sense of urgency and warning, wrapped up in a seemingly innocent amusement ride. The circular motion of the carousel translated nicely into a tight circle that moved with the music, ever scarier, like a machine out of control. Johanna, Kevin, Mark, and Laura nailed the foreboding hand movements perfectly, and I was always left breathless on the final beat. The most satisfying aspect of working with Scott on the choreography for *Brel*, and these two songs in particular, was that it was a truly organic process. We tried things. We researched. We argued over ideas. We consulted the cast. The music was revisited over and over again to insure that everything was timed perfectly and that it continued to make sense, even in the waning days of rehearsal. In the end, I believe those two songs really shone through because of the work and the attention to detail that we gave it. At no point was the message of Brel compromised by the movements of the actors, one of the many things that I am most proud of during my work with New Line.

—Brian Tibbets, co-director

I'm sitting at the piano during one performance of *Jacques Brel* and I'm thinking everything is going really well. The audience is with us and the cast looks like they're having a great time. It's not until after the performance that I find out that Laura has sliced her hand open with a umbrella that had broken during the show's fourth song, "Madeleine." Apparently, she had just sat there and bled until she could get off stage, and then couldn't find a first aid kit. The most impressive thing was that she never missed a beat and it didn't affect her performance in the least. The funniest thing was the next night when we assembled onstage to warm up and we found a dozen or so puddles of dried blood scattered around the stage. Laura examined the spots calmly and then said, "I bet that's a bio-hazard."

—Scott Miller, director

The Ballad of Little Mikey

a St. Louis premiere
Book, Music, and Lyrics by Mark Savage
June 13-28, 1997
St. Marcus Theatre, St. Louis

THE CAST
Mikey—Mike Porter
Steve—Keith Price
Clay—Quenten Schumacher II
David—Ryan Keller
Robert—Kevin Collier
Charles—Tim Kent
Josh—Jim Hannah
Dr. Russo/Murray Cade—Gary Cox

THE ARTISTIC STAFF
Directors—Brian Tibbets and Scott Miller
Directing Intern—Jeffrey Yapp
Costume Designer—Tim Kent
Scenic Designer—Dennis Moore
Lighting Designer—Leif Gantvoort
Props—Jeffrey Yapp
Graphic Design—Tracy Collins

THE BAND
Piano—Scott Miller
Guitar—Mike Bauer
Percussion—Adam Kopff

THE REVIEWS

"When you think you've seen it all, along comes something like *The Ballad of Little Mikey*, the only musical comedy ever to include a number about anonymous sex in a public bathroom...That willingness to poke fun is the sharpest thing about the play."—Judith Newmark, *St. Louis Post-Dispatch*

"Though your jaw may drop, you'll be hard pressed not to smile, for this number ["Tap"], and in fact most of *Little Mikey*, is offered with such a winning spirit that you can't resist...Particularly in the first act, the show is smartly self-mocking, exploring the gay ethos with predictable romantic fawning and some sure, swift kicks."—Mike Isaacson, *The Riverfront Times*

"Scott Miller and his New Line Theatre continue to bring St. Louis challenging, refreshing musical theatre that you simply can't see anywhere else...*The Ballad of Little Mikey* will make you think and it will teach you a thing or two."—Steve Callahan, KDHX-FM

DIRECTOR'S NOTES

Much of the action of *The Ballad of Little Mikey* takes place in 1981, the year Ronald Reagan was elected president. The gay movement had been gaining considerable ground since the historic Stonewall riot of 1969. In 1979 alone, the year leading up to the action of this show, a gay high school senior sued his school for the right to take another boy to prom. The first national gay march on Washington was attended by 100,000 protesters. California Governor Jerry Brown signed an executive order prohibiting anti-gay discrimination in state hiring. Los Angeles became the 44th city to enact gay civil rights legislation. And the Moral Majority was formed by Jerry Falwell to oppose gay rights, pornography, feminism, and communism.

At that time, gay literature was not what it is today. Most gay stories were about how hard it is to be gay, about facing rejection and discrimination, about trying to find love in a world that demonizes homosexuality. Gay characters were not at all like straight characters.

But at some point in the last decade of this millennium, things have really changed for gay Americans. Suddenly, being gay isn't so outrageous. Suddenly, there are gay characters all over mainstream TV. Suddenly, kids are coming out of the closet in high school—some kids today are never even *in* the closet. There are gay high school proms, gay high school students forming gay student clubs, celebrities and politicians (even Republicans) coming out of the closet in record numbers.

And gay literature and theatre have turned a corner. Instead of stories about Being Gay and the pain of being an outcast (as in *The Boys in the Band, La Cage aux Folles*, etc.), stories are now being written about gay characters finding love, building relationships, dealing with family, work, and friendships. Though the main characters are gay, the stories are about facing the same problems and joys straight people face.

The Ballad of Little Mikey embodies both these traditions: the scenes set in 1981 are centered on the issue of being gay and what that means in a hostile world, while the scenes set in the present are about relationships, love, compromise, and sacrifice. In fact, a straight couple could play the scenes in the present without changing a word. *Mikey* not only covers two distinct political and cultural periods, but also two eras in gay literature and theatre. It's interesting to realize that the fantasies the friends express in the song "Ten Percent" are actually coming true—there are gays in the House and the Senate, and people really do take their gay spouses to company picnics now.

Being gay is no longer something to be ashamed of. As a society, we've grown up with Mikey and learned as he did that it's not about who you love; it's about how you love.

REMEMBERING MIKEY

I found the cast album of *Mikey* at Webster Records and fell in love with its honesty, its humor, and its heart. Without too much effort, I got in touch with Mark Savage, who wrote the show, and we had soon made a deal for New Line to produce *Mikey*. The only thing that worried me about staging the show was the song "Tap," an extended, comic musical scene about Mikey discovering the mysteries of gay men having anonymous sex in public bathrooms in the 1970s. How was I going to deal with this number, in which a bunch of gay men do a soft shoe number with their pants around their ankles? But I did what I always do when I'm stumped. I took a step back from it, and my co-director Brian and I asked that all important question, "What is this song about at its core?" I realized this song was about Mikey discovering anonymous sex and finding it altogether unpleasant and unsatisfying. This was an experience he had to go through on his journey to becoming a healthy, well-adjusted, monogamous gay man. I realized the audience had to be led to the same conclusion as Mikey. It had to be slightly disturbing, even though it was a comedy number. I also knew from past experience that if a director is afraid of offending and shies away from presenting a moment on stage honestly, the audience will smell that fear and will inevitably be offended anyway (audiences are kinda like dogs, that way). But if you present that moment honestly, the reaction is generally much better. So we really went for it in "Tap." We simulated every sexual position a person could navigate in a public bathroom. We created a Busby Berkeley-inspired rainbow colored ring of toilet seats. We created an in-your-face, no-holds-barred, admittedly sexual, comedy number, and it worked. Audiences loved it, and few people were offended. Only one person walked out during the entire run. But Mark Savage himself had the funniest reaction. When I asked him what he thought of that number, he told me it was so extreme, so sexual. I laughed and said, "Mark, *you're* the one who wrote a song about anonymous bathroom sex!"

—Scott Miller, director

Extreme Sondheim

◆

a world premiere
Featuring songs from *Anyone Can Whistle, Company, Follies, A Little Night Music, Pacific Overtures, Merrily We Roll Along, Sunday in the Park with George, Into the Woods, Assassins,* and *Passion*
Music and Lyrics by Stephen Sondheim
Conceived by Scott Miller
November 7-22, 1997
St. Marcus Theatre, St. Louis

THE CAST

Chris Brenner, Electa Carlton, Kevin Collier, Gary Cox, Cindy Duggan, Sherry Frank, Keith Hale, Alison Helmer, Lisa Karpowicz, Patrick Kerwin, Jim Merlo, Judy Moebeck, Angela C. (Shultz) Reinert, Dan Sattel, Leo Schloss

THE ARTISTIC STAFF

Director—Scott Miller
Assistant Director—T. Joseph Reinert
Set Decorators—Scott Miller, Dennis Moore, and Greg Hunsaker
Lighting Designer—L.D. Lawson
Lighting Technician—Sara Underwood
Costume Coordinator—Quenten Schumacher II
Graphic Design—Tracy Collins

THE BAND
Piano—Debbie Bernardoni
Trumpet—Paul Hecht
Bass—Terry Kippenberger
Percussion—Adam Kopff

THE REVIEWS

"At New Line Theatre, where *Extreme Sondheim* is now playing, comedy carries the day. The show sparkles in an imaginative trio of comedy songs near the end of the first act…All these songs, with their dazzling lyrics and sophisticated musical style, capture Sondheim's contemporary, New York attitude and are strong enough to work in a revue, stripped of their plot lines."—Judith Newmark, *St. Louis Post-Dispatch*

"For those not familiar with his work, this production will provide a marvelous overview of the work of a talented composer and lyricist. If you are a Sondheim fan, you will relish in sitting back and enjoying an evening of wonderful music presented by a diverse and talented group of performers."—Norma West, KDHX-FM

"What I did realize, hearing the songs out of context this way, was not only how clever and how lyrical Sondheim's songs are, but how *dramatic* they are."—Bob Wilcox, *The Riverfront Times*

DIRECTOR'S NOTES

Stephen Sondheim once said that to be a musician, to live in music, is a gift from God.

Sometimes working on this material became so difficult, so consuming, that we forgot what a gift we had been given—the opportunity to work on, to collaborate on, some of the most brilliant, most emotional, most transforming words and music ever written for the theatre.

Hard-core Sondheim fans often seem like snobs to other musical theatre fans (I've been accused of that myself). It's not intentional. It's a lot like being a wine connoisseur. Once you've experienced the really great stuff, the mediocre stuff is just not satisfying anymore. Once you've wrapped your tongue around the romantic, passionate lyrics in *Passion*, once you've mastered the patter lyrics to "Getting Married Today," once you've sung the glorious dissonances in "The Hills of Tomorrow," nothing else will ever be the same. I know that sounds a bit over-dramatic, but it's really true.

What's so addictive about Sondheim's work is that once you've started exploring its complexities, its subtexts, its great depth, you find that the journey never ends. The more you discover about *Company* or *Passion*, the more you also discover about life, about yourself, about your relationships with those around you. We laugh at "Getting Married Today" in *Company* because we know Amy's fear. Tears come to our eyes when we hear "Loving You" because we've all known the pain of obsessive love.

We hope you can throw yourself into this material the way we have; to hear the jokes, the comic literary references, and the amazing interior rhymes in "Now"; to really hear the fourteen characters who are all talking at the same time in the song "Company"; to laugh at the absurd egotism and heartlessness of Cora in "Me and My Town"; to catch all the subtle digs at organized religion in "The Miracle Song"; to savor the unparalleled beauty of Stephen Sondheim's music.

We hope *Extreme Sondheim* gives you an opportunity to listen to these songs more carefully than you could in their original context, without the distractions of sets and costumes, without having to follow the plot. Just the purity of the words and music.

Some critics have complained that Sondheim is too intellectual and too emotionally distant. I think tonight you'll see how wrong they are.

REMEMBERING EXTREME SONDHEIM

Scott called me one day and asked if I would be willing to be in a concert called *Extreme Sondheim*. I turned him down initially, because I was getting married six days before the opening of the show (which was also my birthday). I reconsidered and agreed to come sing. I was soon to find out what the phrase "art imitates life" really means. When another cast member quit the show, Scott asked me to sing "Getting Married Today" in which Amy spouts all of her fears about getting married and comes up with just about every excuse to get out of it. I must have been asked a million times how in the world I could do that song and be planning my own wedding. My wedding went off without a hitch, the show was well received, but we all know the star of that number was that neon pink veil.

—Angie Shultz

My first show with New Line was *Extreme Sondheim*. I was very excited to work with this company, but also extremely nervous to be working with all these great people who had done numerous shows with New Line already. The first night of rehearsal I remember being simply amazed at how wonderful the ensemble sounded already, and we hadn't even rehearsed at all. As time went along, I started to feel part of the group. I was one of the singers for the song "Someone in a Tree" and I was playing the part of the person under the floor that was listening to what was going on. I noticed that some of the other company members that were watching were starting to laugh during the song. It kept going on during the song and I was starting to wonder if I sounded that bad. After we were over, they said that when I came out on stage and crouched down for the song, it looked like I was a frog about ready to hop around on stage. Needless to say, the rest of the show, they kept calling me The Frog.

—Patrick Kerwin

Two food stories. Well, there was the "cake" incident. I ordered this wonderful cake from McArthur's bakery. The cake decoration was like the cover of the program. Well, to my horror, I did not notice till I brought the cake into the show closing night, that the R was missing. It said "Exteme Sondheim." The joke of the night was, "So where R you?" Everybody started calling me Chis. Then, at the cast party, at my house, Bad Ass Judy (Judy Moebeck) and I made a lovely White Castle paté. People really did not care for it too much; I guess because I used pickle juice instead of white wine for flavoring. Like it would really make a difference. *Extreme Sondheim* was the first time I actually met some of the performers from past New Line shows. I was very intimidated; I thought, "My God, these people are so talented—what can I offer?" But everyone was so wonderful and nice and just fun to be with and so supportive of everyone.

—Chris Brenner, cast member

The Music of Sondheim—A Parody
(To the tune of "The Hills of Tomorrow" from Sondheim's *Merrily We Roll Along*, with parody lyrics by Scott Miller.)

Bemoan the music of Sondheim,
His words too numerous, too.
You'll start to seethe—
There's no time to breathe,
As the lyrics race,
Behold your face turns blue.

Beyond this music, you long for
A simpler musical score…
Just once begin—
You will never win,
As you bust your guts
And wonder what's it for…

March of the Falsettos

---◆---

Book, Music, and Lyrics by William Finn
March 6-14, 1998
St. Marcus Theatre, St. Louis
(playing in a double bill with *Woman with Pocketbook*)

THE CAST
Marvin—Jim Merlo
Whizzer—Chris Brenner
Trina—Deborah Sharn
Mendel—Tim Schall
Jason—Peter Merideth

THE ARTISTIC STAFF
Directors—Scott Miller and Alison Helmer
Assistant Director—T. Joseph Reinert
Choreographer—J.T. Ricroft
Set Designer—Scott Miller
Lighting Designer—L.D. Lawson
Lighting Technician—Sara Underwood
Falsettos Set Pieces—Mark Aeling, MGA Studio
Graphic Design—Tracy Collins

THE BAND
Piano—Scott Miller
Percussion—Adam Kopff

THE REVIEWS

"New Line Theatre's current production of *Falsettos* may be the best work this company has done…Scott Miller and Alison Helmer direct a tight, inventive show with imaginative use of expressionistic images."—Box Wilcox, *The Riverfront Times*

"Angry, challenging work…the New Line performers point up the conflicts within the characters as well as between them."—Gerry Kowarsky, *St. Louis Post-Dispatch*

DIRECTOR'S NOTES

William Finn wrote three one-act musicals about a character (an alter-ego?) named Marvin: *In Trousers*, *March of the Falsettos*, and *Falsettoland*. Later, he and James Lapine combined the second and third chapters into a full-length musical called *Falsettos*, which enjoyed a healthy run on Broadway. So everybody keeps asking me why we're doing just *March of the Falsettos*.

When the two one-acts were combined into one full-length show, they were altered, lyrics changed, things added and deleted, to make this new show more unified, more thematically consistent. So the first half of *Falsettos* became something very different from the one-act *March of the Falsettos*. In the full-length show, both acts are about Marvin and the development of his relationship with his lover Whizzer. The conflict is about whether or not Marvin and Whizzer can build a life together without killing each other first.

But the one-act *March of the Falsettos* is about Marvin and his son Jason. In fact, Jason is the heart of *March*, a boy who needs his father to guide him toward manhood and yet who fears becoming who his father is. The question here is not whether Marvin and Whizzer can stay together. In *March*, Marvin can't sustain relationships with Whizzer, his wife Trina, or his psychiatrist Mendel. Marvin's only salvation is in sustaining his relationship with his son. The one-act isn't about romance; it's about Marvin growing up enough to help Jason grow up. The title of *March of the Falsettos* refers to the journey from childhood, when a boy's voice is soprano, to adulthood, when his voice changes and he becomes a man.

Personally, I think *March of the Falsettos* is a more interesting show, a less conventional musical, a show about deeper, more complicated issues, a show that still deserves to be seen in its original form.

REMEMBERING MARCH OF THE FALSETTOS

I got to work with an incredible cast. Deborah Sharn, whom I had seen in other productions...I was finally going to work with her! I thought at the time: she is a diva goddess. (I do mean that in the good diva sense...are you a good diva or a bad diva?) Then I found out she truly is as wonderful off stage as she is on. I am very thankful to have a rich friendship with her now. Jim Merlo makes everyone look great. He is in the wrong profession. (Deborah and I enjoyed the kisses as much as you, Jim.) I would watch from the wings in amazement of his acting and characterization. He made every character come to life. For me it was the first time I really understood how a song can advance a plot, how to act a song and get to the inner meaning of the lyrics. The whole cast was wonderful to work with and I will never forget them.

—Chris Brenner, "Whizzer Brown"

Woman With Pocketbook

◆

a world premiere
Book and Lyrics by Annie Kessler and Libby Saines
Music by Jeff Blumenkrantz
March 6-14, 1998
St. Marcus Theatre, St. Louis
(playing in a double bill with *March of the Falsettos*)

THE CAST
Doris—Angie (Shultz) Reinert
Dave—Tim Schall
Helen—Cindy Duggan
God—John Ricroft
Angel—Marian Holtz
Angel—Sherry Ingmire
Angel—Mo Monahan
Angel—Renee Sevier

THE ARTISTIC STAFF
Directors—Scott Miller and Alison Helmer
Assistant Director—T. Joseph Reinert
Choreographer—J.T. Ricroft
Set Designer—Scott Miller
Lighting Designer—L.D. Lawson

Lighting Technician—Sara Underwood
Pocketbook Set Pieces—Jack Helmer
Graphic Design—Tracy Collins

THE BAND
Piano—Scott Miller
Percussion—Adam Kopff

THE REVIEWS

"The music by Jeff Blumenkrantz is pleasant, and the lyrics by Annie Kessler and Libby Saines are often very clever. With appealing performances from the New Line cast, *Woman with Pocketbook* adds up to an engaging curtain-raiser [to *March of the Falsettos*]."—Gerry Kowarsky, *St. Louis Post-Dispatch*

"The cast treats this new material well, with really strong comic performances."—Bob Wilcox, *The Riverfront Times*

DIRECTOR'S NOTES

The second half of our evening is a wonderfully whimsical romp through some other compelling issues. New Line held a competition last year for new one-act musicals, a fascinating but almost non-existent genre. Of the twenty-eight shows submitted, *Woman with Pocketbook* was by far the most interesting and the most fun. In this society that values individual liberties as highly as we do, this show asks some interesting questions. What happens when our concept of individual freedom meets the rigid strictures of religion? How much room is there for individual choice in organized religion's view of God and heaven? And, more to the point, is a moral act truly moral if a person is forced into it?

Both *Woman with Pocketbook* and *March of the Falsettos* [the other half of this evening of one-act musicals] are extremely funny and extremely irreverent. Both shows ask some tough questions and leave it to us to sort through the answers, to draw conclusions about love, relationships, family, and God.

And after all, isn't that what theatre does best?

REMEMBERING WOMAN WITH POCKETBOOK

In the spring of 1998, I received a call from a cast member of New Line's *Woman with Pocketbook*. They needed an extra Angel and thought of me. It was my first experience at New Line and I was thrilled to be asked, but wasn't sure what I got myself into. I found out that this Scott Miller guy really isn't dealing with a full deck. I liked that about him, but he was asking the impossible from his "Angels." The libretto called for numerous songs of different languages, one verse in Spanish, one verse in Italian, one in Russian, you name it. I was never sure if it was fake or not. Actually, I was never sure of the lyrics! But I wasn't alone. Angels can be smart. When we didn't know a line we would look at one another in the hopes *somebody* would. We each knew certain sections of the foreign lyrics, and among all of us, we could cover them and everybody thought we actually knew what we were doing.

—Mo Monahan, "Angel"

When I heard about this show and found out that Scott was looking for a "crooner," I knew I had to be a part of it. Besides, how many other chances would I get to play GOD (typecasting of course), especially a God who drinks martinis and smokes cigarettes. Kind of a mix between Frank Sinatra, Dean Martin, and Michael Landon from *Highway to Heaven*. I remember we pondered hard over "What would God wear?" We had discussion after discussion, and then resolved ourselves to taking the most honest way out. A bright red jacket and black slacks! (Yeah, Scott wanted to take the traditional way, as usual.) Well, the reviews came out and there was hell to pay (pah-dum pah). It seemed that the St. Louis theatre—going public didn't want to see God portrayed in this manner, or at least a few reviewers didn't think it was in good taste. In either case, we gave people things to talk about, which is the whole purpose, right? I was glad that some got the joke and went beyond it to get the meaning and the meat of the production. When you die, you don't get to take the "stuff." In the last moments, the only thing that matters is what you have on the inside and not what you have in your pocketbook. It was a relief to know that so many people already knew that.

—John Ricroft, "God," choreographer

It is not often you get the chance to appear in the world premiere of a musical. I found myself as a twenty-four-year-old cast in the role of a sixty-year-old Jewish woman from Brooklyn, but I was so excited to be the lead! I was also terrified to try any accent on the stage, and Scott must have yelled out pronunciations from the piano at me a billion times in rehearsal. When we opened, the show seemed to really connect with many in the audience. It was rewarding to have so many people tell me I reminded them of their mother, their favorite aunt, their crabby neighbor, etc. My gestures onstage and in life became more deliberate, and I learned to stand my ground. Some may consider picking up characteristics of your role as unhealthy, but if you knew Doris, you wouldn't say that. She'd eat you alive.

—Angie Shultz

Assassins

◆

Music and Lyrics by Stephen Sondheim
Book by John Weidman
June 12-27, 1998
St. Marcus Theatre, St. Louis

THE CAST
The Balladeer—Dan Sattel
John Wilkes Booth—David Heimann
Charles Guiteau—Tim Schall
Leon Czolgosz—Kevin Collier
Giuseppe Zangara—Gary Cox
Lee Harvey Oswald—Greg Hunsaker
Samuel Byck—Patrick Kerwin
Sara Jane Moore—Cindy Duggan
Lynette "Squeaky" Fromme—Kirstin Kennedy
John Hinckley—Colin DeVaughan
Shooting Gallery Proprietor—Greg Hunsaker
David Herold—Colin DeVaughan
Florida Bystanders—Patrick Kerwin, Rebecca Hunter
Colin DeVaughan, Dan Sattel, Karin Hansen
Emma Goldman—Karin Hansen
Sara Jane Moore's son, Billy—Rebecca Hunter
President Gerald R. Ford—Greg Hunsaker

THE ARTISTIC STAFF
Directors—Scott Miller, Alison Helmer
Lighting Designer—L.D. Lawson
Lighting Technician—Sara Underwood
Props Coordinator—Greg Hunsaker
Costume Coordinator—Quenten Schumacher
Stage Manager—Amy Francis Schott
Graphic Design—Tracy Collins

THE BAND
Piano—Brad C. Hofeditz
Guitar/Banjo/Harmonica—D. Mike Bauer
Trumpet—Paul Hecht
Percussion—Adam Kopff

THE REVIEWS
"For the most part, 1998 was full of supreme performances in solid productions. Looking back, only New Line Theatre's production of the Stephen Sondheim musical *Assassins* was, as a whole, a wild and gratifying surprise. Here, a talented group of locals inhabited Sondheim's creepy vision of what lives under America's political rocks. It was intense, entertaining, and terrifically 'out there.'"—Mike Isaacson, "1998: The Year in Theater," *The Riverfront Times*

"Intriguing and surprisingly funny...The production—a bare-bones, in-the-round presentation—emphasizes the show's gallows humor and clever lyrics."—Judith Newmark, *St. Louis Post-Dispatch*

"There is a rare, exhilarating thrill to be had for the next two weeks in St. Louis. New Line Theatre's frequently thrilling *Assassins* sets a new standard for the St. Marcus Theatre, and it easily ranks as one of the finest works ever produced there. The evening is funny, disciplined, scary, intimate and strangely credible…The astounding intensity of the cast, and the admirable fact that they never once step 'outside' the material or comment on it, but fully dwell in this strange, murky netherworld, must be credited to the co-direction of Scott Miller and Alison Helmer."—Mike Isaacson, *The Riverfront Times*

DIRECTOR'S NOTES

Many Americans think the men who declare war are strong.
Decisive.

We applauded George Bush for sending troops to the Persian Gulf. And we hailed the men who actually carried out the killing as heroes and patriots. Many Americans also not only accept but actually defend the act of killing criminals.

But we call John Wilkes Booth a traitor and a madman.

Some murder is okay and some murder is not. The murder of Oswald was okay; the murder of JFK was not.

We now know that Abraham Lincoln desecrated the very foundation of our American government in many ways. It is historical fact that he took powers that were not his to take. He ignored—some would say overthrew—the careful construction of the three branches of government designed to hold each other in check, the structure our Founding Fathers so carefully created to avoid tyranny and corruption. He declared war without the approval of Congress. He threw innocent people into jail in both the North and the South without charges and without trials. Many people hated him, in both the North and the South. They believed he was destroying our country.

And yet we think Booth was crazy for thinking he'd be called a hero for killing Lincoln.

Richard Nixon was not unlike Lincoln in some ways. Nixon also trampled on the Constitution. He also took on powers that were not his. He broke the law. He betrayed America. Some would argue that America has never been the same since.

And we think Sam Byck was crazy because he wanted to kill him.

If Lincoln or Nixon had committed these atrocities, these crimes against their nation in any other country on earth, we would call them dictators, despots, tyrants. Many Americans would call for their destruction, their overthrow, maybe even their assassination.

But because Lincoln was murdered, he is remembered as a hero, and more ironically, as a great president. And we make movies about Nixon.

We're not making any statements here about slavery, the Civil War, or Watergate. We're just suggesting that the issues you'll encounter tonight are not as black and white as you might think. The world is a more complicated place than our stories, textbooks, newspapers, movies, and CNN Headline News would have us believe. (Check out a book called *American Assassins: The Darker Side of Politics* by James W. Clarke for more on that topic.)

These assassins are not insane. (Okay, except for Guiteau.) The accusations leveled by Booth, Byck, Czolgosz and others are true. We must listen to them, if for no other reason than the simple fact that if we do not learn from history, we are doomed to repeat it.

REMEMBERING ASSASSINS

I played Sam Byck and one of the scenes calls for Byck to be driving a car and eating a hamburger. Because of his anger, he throws the burger out the car window. When we did the performance, it was done in the round, so when I threw out the burger, I threw it out into the audience. I had to make sure that I cleared the heads of the audience. Well, let's just say, this was not always easy. The first night I did it in rehearsal, I hit one of the cast members in the head! As time went on, I got more proficient and things went off without a hitch until the second week of performances. Because we had sold out shows, Scott decided to add some extra seats at the last minute and added them along the wall at which I usually threw the burger. I didn't know until the show started that he had added the seats. The whole time before the scene, I was thinking about where I was going to throw the burger without hitting anyone. I thought I had found a place; however, people decided to move their seats during the performance. I did the scene and threw the burger and didn't think anymore about it. As we came out after the show, a person came up to me and said, "Hey, here is your hamburger. You threw it right in my lap!"

—Patrick Kerwin, "Sam Byck"

This is such an awesome show. I was lucky enough to be a part of it both times New Line performed this extraordinary work of Sondheim's, as Zangara the first time and as the Balladeer the second time. I thought doing it in the round really added to the intimacy and in-your-face nature of the show and helped us achieve something that I believe Sondheim would have been proud of. These were some highlights for me: the duet between Kirsten Kennedy and Colin DeVaughan on "Unworthy of Your Love." It was beautiful each and every night. Kevin Collier's Czolgosz. Kevin's performance really *coooooooked* and he has since secured his place in my mind as the epitome of a scary, angry Russian man. (Ivan Drago eat your heart out!) Gary Cox as Zangara. Gary makes more faces on stage than anyone I know. He is so much fun to watch if only to see what his face is going to do!

—Dan Sattel, "Balladeer"

I played Sara Jane Moore, the part that will live in infamy. I *loved* doing that role, though there is one particular scene that is an actor's nightmare. It includes eating, drinking, smoking, guns and voluminous props—all while talking of course—and one night the seat split open on my real 1970s pants when I sat down. Luckily I had on a long 70s vest which covered the split—which was lucky because the theatre was *so* hot that none of us wore underwear. Also, the show's publicity picture of me eating Kentucky Fried Chicken and drinking the Tab soda was literally splattered in every newspaper in town for weeks until everyone

was sick of looking at it! However, every place I go, even now, someone will come up and say, "Wow, you were *so* good in *Assassins!*"—sometimes people I don't even know. Occasionally, our esteemed director, Scott Miller, is present when this happens, and he says, "Gee, that's great, but there were *other* people in the show too!"
—Cindy Duggan, "Sara Jane Moore"

My character, Sam Byck, has two monologues during the show, one of them while sitting on a park bench, having lunch and making tape recordings to send to important people so they can hear his message. While I know that many people tell stories of people talking in the audience, I got my first real taste of it during the first week of performances. There was an older gentleman who I think was a bit hard of hearing who thought that my character was really funny. However, he also had a hard time hearing some of what I was saying, since we were doing the show in the round and at times I was not looking at him while doing my lines. During the whole monologue, I could hear the guy making very loud statements like "That guy is really funny," "He is right about that," and "Oh, my, that is good." However, when he couldn't hear me, he kept asking his wife "What did he say?" Eventually, because he was talking so loud, people started to laugh at him and were whispering about The Loud Guy. I kept going and didn't forget too many of my lines, but I will never forget trying to compete with the audience member for attention.
—Patrick Kerwin, "Sam Byck"

My favorite moment in the show was one I created. It may be the moment I'm most proud of in any show I've done. The second to last scene finds all the assassins from all times coming together in the Texas Book Depository to convince Oswald to shoot Kennedy—truly chilling stuff. Then when Oswald pulls the trigger, there's an instrumental segue in the style of Aaron Copland's music, and it segues directly into the finale, "Everybody's Got the Right to Be Happy." My addition was that during the instrumental segue, I sent each assassin out into the audience. I told them each to pick two or three people and tell those people—quietly, privately, intimately—why they *had* to kill the president. I told the actors they could use lines from the show or make things up, but to really try to *convince* the audience. I wanted everyone in the audience to be experiencing something different at this moment, hearing only one or two actors, wondering what the others were saying. Every night, the audience was mesmerized, their eyes glued to the assassin nearest them, hanging on every word. And every night, the last one to finish was Tim Schall as Guiteau, one of the truly insane assassins. And the last words that rang in the air before the finale were Guiteau quietly hissing "I did it for *you!* I did it for *you!*" It was the most disturbing moment I've ever created in the theatre.

—Scott Miller, director

Out of Line Productions Presents

Party

◆

a St. Louis premiere
a comedy by David Dillon
August 6–29, 1998
St. Marcus Theatre, St. Louis

THE CAST
Kevin—Ted Cancila
Ray—Brad L. Graham
Philip—Michael A. Naggi
Brian—Bobby Grosser
Peter—Thomas Long
James—Walter Marts
Andy—Matthew Miley

THE ARTISTIC STAFF
Director—Scott Miller
Set Designer—Dennis Moore
Lighting Designer—Sara Underwood
Props Coordinator—Dennis Moore
Costume Coordinator—Quenten Schumacher
Graphic Design—Tracy Collins

THE REVIEWS

"*Party* is consistently amusing and frequently hilarious."—Gerry Kowarsky, *St. Louis Post-Dispatch*

"*Party* is light, funny, and mildly shocking if you're not scandalized by full frontal male nudity and lots of it...*Party* is also innocent—it means no harm and does no harm. It celebrates friendship, tolerance, acceptance of self and others, and freedom from unhealthy inhibition."—Harry Weber, *The Riverfront Times*

DIRECTOR'S NOTES

Out of Line Productions was created so that New Line could occasionally work on projects that fall outside the scope of our usual focus on issue-oriented musicals and revues. We didn't want to change New Line's fundamental identity, so we created this new branch of the company. We hope you enjoy our experiment.

Party may seem at first to be pretty lightweight compared to what we usually do (shows like *Sweeney Todd, Passion, Assassins, March of the Falsettos*), but I'm not sure it really is. In a sense, *Party*'s very existence is a political statement. Living room comedy (or drawing room comedy, as it was once called) has been exclusively heterosexual since Oscar Wilde (ironically enough) and even before that. Certainly in 1998 there's no excuse for that. Theatre is supposed to reflect and comment on the world around us, and gay people have living rooms too.

Sure, there have been gay plays like *The Boys in the Band* and *Love! Valour! Compassion!*, but those are plays *about* being gay, about how hard it is to be gay, about how gay people suffer at the hands of an unfeeling straight world, blah, blah, blah. *Party* isn't about being gay. It's about love, friendship, sex, God, marriage, loss, and loyalty, all the things the other living room comedies are about. These aren't gay issues—they're human issues.

It's also about one of the most compelling of human needs—the need to find your tribe, to inherit your culture, to know where you come from and where you're headed. While African-Americans, Italian-Americans, and Irish-Americans are born into their tribes, gay people have to seek out theirs. Establishing that connection may be a different process for gay Americans, but the need and the feelings of belonging are the same. In many ways, the older characters in *Party* pass on their culture to the younger characters the same way Tevye and Golde pass on their culture to their children in *Fiddler on the Roof.*

What attracted me most to *Party* was that being gay is never an issue for these characters—and that's the way it should be. These characters never ask for our pity for being gay, and they never expect special points for being an Oppressed People. Some of these guys are really nice guys. Some are obnoxious. And we judge them by their words and actions, not by their battle scars or the prejudices they may have faced. Again, as it should be.

My hope is that this play is just as much fun, just as true to life, just as touching to straight people as it is to gay people. These are not gay characters; they are people for whom being gay is one part of their identities. For Ray, the Catholic priest in the play, he is a priest first, a teacher second, and a gay man third.

Maybe someday soon, plays will stop being "straight plays" or "gay plays" and they can just be *good* plays. Meanwhile, we hope you enjoy your evening with the guys in *Party*. They're all having too much fun to deal with any heavy issues and we hope you will too.

REMEMBERING PARTY

Here's how it went down: I came to a casting call to provide moral support for my ex, who was going to try out for a play, *Party*. Coincidentally, I had gone through a personal health scare and when that turned out to be harmless, I felt daring. So when the ex bagged the audition, I decided to step up to the plate—something I had always wanted to do. It was my first audition, and first acting assignment, ever. And, it was a big, successful 'naked play'—certainly diving into the deep end of the theatrical pool my first time at bat; and something of a departure for staid St. Louis. But *Party* was more than a comedic romp—it was pivotal for me personally. Not only did I get my feet wet theatrically, I got to meet some people who remain important to me in my adult life to this day. The audiences who saw *Party* saw eight men acting like friends; in real life, it was much the same—bickering, off-key singing, throwing non-sequiturs around. And even if I did hear the occasional snicker in the audience when my character's supposed age (I played the part of a 23-year-old when I was, ahem, thirty-something), the experience was a blast. *Party* opened other doors for me—it helped me get back on track creatively. I finished a book. I wrote a play. I started to syndicate a column. Although I was bitten once by the acting bug, I have now recovered—after all, with so much exposure in *Party*, anything else is going to be a bit bare. Pun intended. New Line Theatre is a company that takes some chances: on people, and on productions. That is a good thing. Scott Miller is a master at helping push buttons—another good thing. I'm happy I was one of those buttons, and a part of the New Line history. We were, at the time, ready to give a *Party* that nobody might attend. Happily, that did not happen, and it was a great Party indeed. Thank you, New Line. And Happy Birthday.

—Thomas Long, "Peter"

Once we decided to produce *Party*, my first worry was how we would find seven men who could act and didn't mind getting naked on stage. Then as I prepared for auditions, my second worry was whether or not we should ask them to get naked at auditions. I talked to my board, to friends, to other directors, and everyone pretty much agreed we had to ask them to disrobe at auditions, to make sure it didn't freak them out too badly and that they could still act with their clothes off. But this was uncharted territory for me. We finally decided we'd have a regular first audition, then tell them they'd have to get naked at the callbacks. We did a group callback and one by one, they'd get up on stage, do their monologue, take off their clothes, and do the monologue again. During each monologue the same thing kept running through my mind: "Be professional. Look at their eyes. Be professional. Look at their eyes. Be professional…" Surprisingly, most of them stayed naked after they came off stage, so that by the end of the evening, we had a theatre full of naked men lounging around like…like…like they weren't naked! It was the most bizarre experience of my career. Though not entirely unpleasant…

—Scott Miller, director

Songs for a New World

◆

a St. Louis premiere
Music and Lyrics by Jason Robert Brown
Conceived by Daisy Prince
October 30–November 14, 1998
St. Marcus Theatre, St. Louis

THE CAST
Christopher Brenner, John Rhine, Deborah Sharn, Kimi Short

THE ARTISTIC STAFF
Directors—Scott Miller, Alison Helmer
Music Director—Scott Miller
Lighting Designer—Jamie Brink
Scenic Painter—Heather Bennett
Lighting Technician—Amy Francis Schott
Box Office Manager—Steve Dohrmann
Graphic Design—Tracy Collins

THE BAND
Piano—Scott Miller
Guitar—D. Mike Bauer
Bass—Terry Kippenberger
Percussion—Adam Kopff

THE REVIEWS

"*Songs for a New World* is that very rare beast: an abstract musical...Here is a musical that doesn't try to bombard or cajole you—it simply speaks honestly through fine music and proves that less can most certainly be more...Individually, the performers are fine, together they are fabulous, and the harmonies and group singing are uncommonly rich and vibrant...The mystical union of song and performance was simply profound at the St. Marcus...a true theatrical gem."—Mike Isaacson, *The Riverfront Times*

"I'm at a loss as to just what to call this production, except fascinating, engrossing, and totally absorbing. It's the kind of performance that just cries out to be seen more than once, just to get all the nuances of the lyrics of the songs. Maybe one could call this a musical call to personal reflection, almost a contemporary worship service without dogmatics, but even that might be too limiting a description for such a freewheeling exploration into the human soul...The voices of the cast members are all outstanding, and the emotion they put into each piece lifts the presentation from just a bunch of songs into something between poetry and worship. Most of the time the message is a powerful message of hope and faith in a God who knows the future, but sometimes it becomes a picture of the despair that comes when one loses that hope and faith. It is, as you can tell, a complex and fascinating evening you'll be thinking about for a long time to come. Come see the presentation with a friend whose opinion you value, then plan to spend many invigorating hours talking about what you heard on stage."—Russ Thomas, KDHX-FM

"*Songs for a New World*, a song-cycle by Jason Robert Brown, has neither [cabaret nor musical theatre] structure—nor any other. The unsurprising result: a fairly shapeless production."—Judith Newmark, *St. Louis Post-Dispatch*

"Just as personally inspiring for me was watching five local actors pour their hearts and talents into *Songs for a New World*, another New Line production, featuring the fine songs of Jason Robert Brown...making for a truly cherished memory."—Mike Isaacson, "1998: The Year in Theatre," *The Riverfront Times*

DIRECTOR'S NOTES

I didn't love the original cast album of *Songs for a New World* when I first bought it a couple years ago. I didn't get it. But the more I listened, the more I realized there was so much there worth getting.

Like *Jacques Brel is Alive and Well and Living in Paris* (which New Line produced in 1997), this is a show that is kind-of a revue, kind-of a song cycle, kind-of a concept musical. It almost *dares* you to figure it all out. But that's what was so exciting about *Jacques Brel*, the challenge to direct the show intelligently and clearly enough, and to perform the songs well enough that the audience would be able to understand everything. And it helps that what may be confusing on the CD can be much clearer when the audience can see the performers, see their faces, their body language, costumes, etc.

And yet, even with the help of visual clues, these are not songs that lay out at the beginning everything you need to know. You have to listen. You have to accept that these characters may be distorting the truth, intentionally or not. But when you do listen closely, the rewards are great in this show. When you realize that the woman in "I'm Not Afraid of Anything" has just walked out on her husband, her claims of courage and adventure take on a much darker tint. When you realize that the young woman in "Christmas Lullaby" has just found out she's pregnant (and no doubt completely alone), her sweet lullaby becomes more a bittersweet anthem of determination and a newfound realization of self-worth. When you realize the soldier in "Flying Home" has died in battle, this powerful hymn becomes both sad and joyful.

And what ties all these independent songs into a unified evening of theatre is their one common theme. In every song, someone faces that moment in life when everything is going perfectly and suddenly disaster strikes, in the form of the loss of a job, an unexpected pregnancy, the death of a loved one, the end of a marriage, imprisonment, even suicide. As the opening says:

It's about one moment,
That moment you think you know where you stand.
...
But then the earthquake hits
Then the bank closes in
Then you realize you didn't know anything.
Nobody told you the best way to steer
When the wind starts to blow.

But it's even more about *surviving* those moments. In each song, a character truly finds himself in a "new world," a world in which the old rules no longer apply, in which everything he thought he knew about life has to be figured out all over again. We've all been there. But we survive.

The finale says, "Hear my song. It was made for the times when you don't know where to go." And that's what this show is about, to remind us that we all go through these times, and almost always, we come out on the other end still in one piece. We are survivors. And we are never really alone.

REMEMBERING SONGS FOR A NEW WORLD

Performing in *Songs For A New World* was probably the most terrifying and exciting theatrical experience I've had. At one point in rehearsals my mantra was, "Fear is a motivating factor." I knew also that I wasn't the only one terrified by the challenges presented in this amazing musical revue by Jason Robert Brown. Scott had his work cut out for him in finding an African-American tenor who could sing to the stars. He did find that in the amazing John Rhine, who floored all of us with his bluesy, sweet gospel sound. For my part in the show I needed to create a German accent, a New York Jewish accent—a distinct character for each song, not to mention having to sing alto for the first time. I'd been spoiled always singing lead. I was up for the challenge. My favorite song to perform was "Surabaya Santa," a takeoff of the song "Surabaya Johnny." Perched atop a cabaret chair, in a housecoat and slippers, I was this crazed, alcoholic, sex-starved German-born wife of Santa Claus who suffered badly from North Pole cabin fever and threatened Santa with running off with his elves. My inspiration for the song came from a local stage mother who drinks a wee bit and whose lipstick often runs beyond the lines of her lips. Each night I reveled in performing this song, but I knew that the next time we did the show I would have to wrestle Chris Brenner (my wonderful co-performer) for the song, as he was a perfect candidate for it.

—Deborah Sharn, cast member

One of the hardest mother-f—-ing shows I have ever done in my life, but I loved every minute. Normally when you leave the stage after a song, you can rest and regroup and relax a little bit. Not in this show. The music was so difficult that we could not let up for one minute. But I think all the effort was worth it. The saddest part of the show was the lack of audience. I don't think that mattered to the cast—we loved the show, we loved doing the music, and we enjoyed working with each other. I think it was wonderful that the cast got to sing some of that great music at the concert at the Sheldon. An audience finally heard our song.

—Chris Brenner, cast member

(Two weeks into rehearsals for *Songs for a New World*.)
ALISON: Hey, Scott. What on earth are we gonna do with the song "On the Deck of a Spanish Sailing Ship"?
SCOTT: I don't know…we'll worry about that later.
(Four weeks later)

ALISON: Hey, Scott. What on earth are we gonna do with "On the Deck of a Spanish Sailing Ship"?
SCOTT: I don't know...we'll worry about that later.
    (A week and a half before opening night)
ALISON: Hey, Scott. What on earth are we gonna do with "On the Deck of a Spanish Sailing Ship"?
SCOTT: I don't know...we'll worry about that later.
    (Final dress rehearsal. "Deck" has just ended, finally staged, and ALISON, who has tears of happiness, joy, and relief in her eyes, turns to SCOTT, who also has tears in his eyes.)
SCOTT: Damn! We're good.

                                            —Alison Helmer, co-director

I was really sick during *Songs for a New World*. I had been getting migraines for years, but by November of 1998, I had had one continuous migraine for five months. I didn't have health insurance, so I hadn't been to a doctor. The show was one of the hardest I had ever worked on; I had foolishly decided to play the monstrous score for the performances myself, and I was feeling awful. Three nights before opening night, I missed a rehearsal for the second time in my life. I just couldn't get out of bed. Somehow, I managed to pull myself together and I played every performance, sometimes wondering if I was going to pass out during the next song. Most nights, I went home and straight to bed after the show. The week after we closed, I finally gave in, after not being able to eat for two days. I called my co-director and friend, Alison, at 5:00 a.m. on the Sunday after Thanksgiving and asked her to take me to the emergency room, where they discovered I had blood pressure of 230 over 140. They thought I was going to have a stroke any minute, or that I had just had one. They admitted me and three days later I was fine. I realize now how true that old line is: The show must go on. My body didn't give out on me until after the show had closed. It knew.

                                              —Scott Miller, director

My first experience with New Line Theatre was seeing *Assassins*. Because of the quality of performances, I knew I had to work for this theatre company, which led to me to audition for *Songs for a New World*. I sang an excerpt of "Christmas Lullaby" during the audition, and it was beautiful. I wanted to sing the entire piece and learn its meaning. Deborah Sharn was there to audition as well, and all I could think about was how fantastic it would be to do a show with someone of such high caliber. A week later when Scott Miller called (I had already given up hope) to ask me to do the show, I was ecstatic. I am going to work with Deborah Sharn (who I referred to as the Great Deborah Sharn), this amazing theatre company who put on *Assassins*, and I get to sing the beautiful song! Does it get any better? It does. The weeks ahead would unfold incredible melodies and harmonies, beautiful songs and stories about people, a level of performance, strength, and inner being I never knew I had, and best of all, a very special friendship to last a lifetime, a unique relationship all our own. Deborah, Chris, John, Scott, Alison, Amy are all in my soul and spirit forever, and we know without words how we are a part of each other every time we meet. From the opening sequence to "Hear My Song" at the end, we took an amazing journey together, each moment as incredible as the next. I wonder what new meanings these stories will take on for me several years from now. Maybe we'll have the privilege to take the journey once again.

—Kimi Short, cast member

Camelot

◆

Book and Lyrics by Alan Jay Lerner
Music by Frederick Loewe
March 11–27, 1999
St. Marcus Theatre, St. Louis

THE CAST

Arthur Pendragon—Ted Cancila
Guenevere—Deborah Sharn
Lancelot du Lac—Karl E. Berberich
Merlyn/Pellinore—Steve Johnson
Sir Dinadan—Kevin Collier
Sir Lionel—Keith Thompson
Sir Sagramore—Jesse Lawder
Sir Castor—Jerry Smith
Sir Gawaine/Mordred—Walter Marts
Nimué/Lady Catherine—Kimi Short
Morgan Le Fay/Lady Elaine—Rebecca Hunter
Lady Anne/Tom of Warwick—Sarah Laak
Lady Sybil—Johanna Schloss

THE ARTISTIC STAFF

Directors—Scott Miller, Alison Helmer
Music Director—Scott Miller

Lighting Designer—Jamie Brink
Costume Designer—Elizabeth Krausnick
Technical Director—Karl Berberich
Lighting Technician—Sara Epstein
Stage Manager—Amy Francis Schott
Weapons Designer—Bryan Fick
Box Office Manager—Steve Dohrmann
Graphic Design—Laura Aeling

THE BAND
Piano—Steven C. Showalter
Guitar/Mandolin—D. Mike Bauer
Trumpet—Paul Hecht
Percussion—Adam Kopff

THE REVIEWS

"This show does not look, sound, or feel like any other *Camelot* [but]…this stripped down version has a lot going for it."—Judith Newmark, *St. Louis Post-Dispatch*

"It's a longish evening, but so full of fine voices and serious, convincing performances, that its command of our attention is unfailing."—Steve Callahan, KDHX-FM

"The musical's dark ending doesn't jar against too light and romantic a tone in the earlier scenes. Elemental passions and their potential for trouble lurk in the first moments, when even wise Merlin succumbs to the seductions of the flesh."—Bob Wilcox, *The Riverfront Times*

DIRECTOR'S NOTES

Why *Camelot*? For a company known for doing *Assassins, Sweeney Todd,* and *Out on Broadway*, it seems a strange choice.

Well, I've been answering that question for a year now. And the answer keeps changing. It seems now there are two answers.

First, I'm crazy. And so is everyone who works with me.

Second, *Camelot* is a masterpiece. It deals with some extremely heavy issues, all still relevant, with surprising parallels to our current scandal-ridden government [with Bill Clinton and Monica Lewinksy]. And its themes of sex, violence, betrayal, and death are the same themes we've explored in our other work.

What we discovered was that this story and these characters have a complexity and a depth that has been lost or ignored over the years. Going back to the source, *The Once and Future King*, we found richer, deeper characters than we'd ever seen in this show before, characters the original production no doubt explored fully but that have been forgotten and simplified over time. *Camelot* is no fairy tale. It's a fiery, tragic, thought-provoking fable that somehow manages to make us laugh along the way.

But though it's a masterpiece, it's one with flaws and that makes it a tremendous challenge. How do you make an audience care about Arthur who continually refuses to face the obvious dangers that lurk behind every corner of his court? Or Guenevere, who has the gentlest, most caring husband in the world, and leaves him for another man? And what about Lancelot, who sleeps with his best friend's wife?

The answer is to explore *why* Arthur ignores the signs, what is missing in Arthur and Guenevere's marriage, what Guenevere needs that Arthur can't give her and that Lance can, and how Lance can balance his obsessive love for Arthur and his passionate love for Guenevere. This is a show about passions—Arthur's passion for the philosophy of law and for changing the world, Guenevere's passion for life and romance, Lancelot's passion for Arthur's dream and for Guenevere's love.

Ours is a muscular, aggressive, confrontational *Camelot*, one that lives not in the world of musical comedy, but instead in the dark world of Arthur, King of the Britons, and his knights of the Round Table. This is one of the greatest legends of the western world. We hope that we have brought to it the power and depth of understanding that it deserves.

As with all our shows, what we're attempting requires more from you, the audience, than most musicals ask, but we hope that the rewards for your efforts will be considerable. Enjoy.

REMEMBERING CAMELOT

For years, I had wanted to do *Camelot* small. Intimate, close up, psychological, personal. I wanted to get rid of the stupid dances, the idiotic costume parades, all the crap that had nothing to do with the story. The original production had cost *over a million dollars* and that was in 1960! But the story is really about just three people—people with Shakespearean-sized passions, sure, but at their core, *real* people with *real* feelings, real insecurities, and best of all, real contradictions. These are complicated, flawed, fascinating characters. I had played Arthur in high school and knew that there was more in that material than most people saw—or would admit they saw. I was convinced that for *Camelot* to really work, it had to be small and private. The audience had to feel like eavesdroppers, not spectators at a parade. I asked the three leads to make every scene personal and unbearably vulnerable, to rarely open themselves up physically to the audience (the usual practice in musicals), and above all, to let the show be unashamedly sexual and passionate. I'd like to think all these unusual—some said "radical"—ideas paid off, that our *Camelot* was not only different, but better. But my greatest joy was hearing audience members leaving the theatre each night, saying that they hadn't remembered *Camelot* being that funny. Or sexy. Or sad. The biggest lesson I've learned with New Line is that the original production of a show isn't always the best way to do it. In some cases, the authors were bound by convention, by finances, by audience expectations, by fear—and they didn't always do their work justice. And sometimes it takes the distance of a few decades to see that.

—Scott Miller, director

I walked into the basement of the St. Marcus Theatre, not having a clue what to expect. Hey, I'm still pretty new to the theatre, and I had no concept of what Professional Non-Equity Theatre was. But I was prepared. I had my sheet music for "If Ever I Would Leave You" under my arm when a large—no, gigantic—man greeted me at the door. Intimidating first impression? Definitely. I filled out my audition sheet, and almost wet myself when I saw that there would be pay involved. Who knew a person could get paid for doing something this fun? Well, I got up there and sang my little baritone heart out, stone cold stiff with fright. The blond guy at the piano, who I gathered was the director, then tested my range and seemed pleasantly surprised at the depth of it, commenting that my range was the one he wished he had. I didn't know quite what to make of this, but stayed around to read anyway (but not dance…hmmm…in *Camelot*?). They asked me to read for Lancelot. Shocking, to say the least. After all, I was only seventeen. So, I put on my pseudo-French accent after asking if such a thing would be necessary, and went to work. I think the thing that threw me the most was that there was no Arthur to grovel to. Just me, on a bare stage, blind as a bat, on my knees towards the invisible king. I think the scariest part of that audition, though, was the thought that I might actually be cast as Lancelot. Fortunately, as the story goes, a fabulous baritone named Karl came along and snatched the part with one vocal chord tied around his back. I was so relieved to be a knight, I even offered to sing tenor (but that's a whole other chapter).

—Jesse Lawder, "Sir Sagramore"

For me, one of the funniest parts of the show was something the audiences were never aware of. It's at the end of the joust. Kevin Collier's character is killed, carried on stage and then brought back to life by Lancelot. It's a very emotional scene in the show. The funny part was watching Jerry, Walter, Jesse and Keith carry Kevin from the back of the theatre to the stage. Kevin is at least six feet twelve inches tall and weighs…a lot. Each night when they struggled to carry him on the stretcher to the stage, my mind would always go back to the night they dropped him on his head during rehearsal. Kevin wasn't too happy about being dropped. In fact, the last time I heard that much cursing from one human being was when my ex-wife was giving birth. Thank goodness Kevin wasn't hurt and there was no permanent damage to the stage.

—Steve Johnson, "King Pellinore"

My favorite memory of *Camelot* was a moment we had backstage. For the first weekend of the run, all the Lords and Ladies spent their downtime chatting in the green room together. For no known reason, by the second weekend, the women had begun to retreat to our dressing room and left the men in the green room alone. We prided ourselves on having plenty of time to make transitions upstairs through the sanctuary of the St. Marcus to cross over and enter through the back of the theatre. But one night, we were involved in our conversation and hearing a cue, suddenly realized we were in grave danger of missing our entrance at the back of the theatre. Well, the "Queens of the Manor" (and I do mean *queens*) were quite bitter about their ladies doing their own thing, so they fell into a laughing heap as the four of us burst open the dressing room door looking like a pack of flying nuns in our long Medieval ware and raced up the back stairs, tripping and falling on each other's clothes.

—Beck Hunter, "Morgan Le Fay, Lady Elaine"

I didn't think there was a spot for me in *Camelot*, but Scott told me about Nimué. He described her as an enchantress that sings this one beautiful song, which was enough reason for me to audition! Steve Johnson played Merlin and it was my job as Nimué to seduce him away. Steve was great to work with on and off stage. Our scene together was short but beautiful, and I enjoyed it very much. Much to my surprise, Joe Pollack complimented me in his review in *Backstage,* and Judith

Newmark gave me a year-end Judy Award as one of the Best Supporting Actresses of the year. I appreciate the compliments very much, but I can't help chuckling about it because I was only onstage for about two minutes! Deborah, Ted, and Karl were terrific and this was their show, but we enjoyed watching and playing our parts in the story. It was always fun watching the invisible horses race towards each other in the jousts and "seeing" Lancelot's victories, especially the time they dropped Sir Dinadan (Kevin) while carrying him back to Arthur. Well, at least it was fun for us!

—Kimi Short, "Nimué"

The very first show I costumed for the New Line Theatre was *Camelot*. At that time their productions were in the basement of the St. Marcus on Russell Avenue. I remember my first reaction when I descended the steps and walked through the black hanging curtains to the theatre space: *this is as low as I can get*. The atmosphere was dark and close due to the low ceiling, soft lighting, and the pillars scattered throughout the seating area. However, throughout that first pre-production time and during the performances, I found out that the theatre company isn't about the space [in which it performs], but the people who make up the company. We all joked about the size of the roaches in the green room (while I kept my feet off the floor), and the dressing rooms were cozy, not cramped. I actually felt comforted when I'd walk backstage by the Christmas lights and the hot, glowing boiler. But I found that the best part of it all was the genuine thanks and gratitude I received from the actors when I costumed them. They treated me and my costumes very well. Even though the company has had to change venues with the closing of the St. Marcus, the same camaraderie has continued. It's such a warm feeling to get applause from the people I costume, for they know that I do it so they can be better in their roles, and that I do the best that I can do. What more could I ask for?

—Betsy Krausnick, costumer

New Line's production of *Camelot* was superb, provocative, delightful and yet so remarkably different from any other version I've ever seen of this show. As I sat in the audience that evening, I found it difficult to believe that my adult son, Scott Miller, was directing this highly sophisticated show. It seemed such a short time ago that Scott, my lanky young teenager, starred as the ill-fated King in his high school production of *Camelot*. My pride in his directing skills almost equaled those I experienced as I watched him perform so many years ago. Anyone who is a mother will understand my feelings…the rest of you will just have to grin and bear it.

—Joan Zobel, mother of the director

Then there was the time when everyone got late night phone calls.

I had rehearsal one night, around January or February, and my ex-girlfriend was in town from school. She and I were good friends still, and we decided to go out for coffee or something after I got out of rehearsal. So, as I got out, she picked me up and off we went on our way to a fun night. It was, of course, a school night, and I did stay out quite late. I got home around two to find my father and his fiancée not in sight. Well, the way the story goes, they woke up to my empty bed, and happened to find my *Camelot* cast list. They then proceeded to make calls to at least three people (including the directors, Scott and Alison) wondering if we were still in rehearsal and if they had any idea where I might be. Seeing as how rehearsal got out at ten and it was now two, no one really had much to say on that subject. Needless to say, I had a lot of explaining to do next rehearsal.

—Jesse Lawder, "Sir Sagramore"

In Act II of *Camelot*, Sarah, Beck, Kimi, and I were offstage a lot (which is generally the case for any woman in *Camelot* who isn't Guenevere). On one particular night, we apparently had been listening to the same radio station on the way to the theatre, for we all had The

Bangles' version of "Hazy Shade of Winter" in our heads. Very softly, almost in a whisper, we sang it and split into the harmonies as though we had rehearsed it for months. We decided we'd make a great girl band. And we ate a lot of grapefruit. In case you were wondering what we did for that hour backstage before the finale…
—Johanna Schloss, "Lady Sybil"

Into the Woods

♦

Music and Lyrics by Stephen Sondheim
Book by James Lapine
June 10–26, 1999
St. Marcus Theatre, St. Louis

THE CAST

Narrator/Mysterious Man—Steven R. Johnson
Cinderella—Sarah Laak
Jack—Adam Eisen
Jack's Mother—Cindy Duggan
Baker—Robb Kennedy
Baker's Wife—Deborah Sharn
Cinderella's Stepmother—Rebecca Hunter
Cinderella's Stepsister, Florinda—Christina Rios
Cinderella's Stepsister, Lucinda—Johanna Schloss
Steward—Justin Heinrich
Little Red Ridinghood—Kate Novak
Witch—Laura Beard Aeling
Cinderella's Mother/Granny/Giant's Wife—Mary "Mo" Monahan
Wolf/Cinderella's Prince—Karl E. Berberich
Rapunzel—Kimi Short
Rapunzel's Prince—Sean Pritchett

THE ARTISTIC STAFF
Directors—Scott Miller & Alison Helmer
Music Director—Scott Miller
Set Designer & Scene Painter—Karl Berberich
Costume Designers—Theresa Doggett & Tim Kent
Lighting Designer—Jamie Brink
Lighting Technician—Sara Epstein
Stage Manager—Amy Francis Schott
Box Office Manager—Steve Dohrmann
Graphic Design—Laura Beard Aeling & Zachary Lips

THE BAND
Piano—Brad Hofeditz
Trumpet—Paul Hecht
Flute—Jessie Poepping
Percussion—Adam Kopff

THE REVIEWS

"With *Into the Woods*, [Miller] continues his experiments in proportion. His intimate production of Stephen Sondheim's sophisticated fairy tale reduces the Broadway hit to a nursery scale, befitting both its subject matter and its psychoanalytic viewpoint. The production…makes the most of the St. Marcus Theatre, turning its small size into an asset…*Into the Woods* brings together an exceptionally consistent cast."—Judith Newmark, *St. Louis Post-Dispatch*

"You can savor those words and music [of *Into the Woods*] in what may be New Line's finest production yet…The cast plays with smart assurance, without a weak link in the chain…The whole production turns these old tales into adult versions rich in wit, music, and emotion—the most satisfying kind of entertainment."—Bob Wilcox, *The Riverfront Times*

DIRECTOR'S NOTES

At each stage of his life, a child may take different lessons from a single fairy tale. Each time he hears in it some new insight or lesson, depending on his needs at that moment in life. Perhaps at one moment, the child will learn that we must follow our parents' instructions when he reads or hears *Little Red Ridinghood*. At a later moment, he may take from it the idea that life is full of dangers and adventures, but that no matter how scary it may get, we generally come out all right on the other end of even the darkest moments.

But fairy tales are for children. Well, maybe. Wouldn't it be foolish to assume that just because we're adults, we have nothing left to learn? In fact, *Into the Woods* is a fairy tale for adults. Real fairy tales divide the world into Good and Bad, with no gray area in between. Real fairy tales leave no room for moral ambiguity. *Into the Woods* takes us, as adults, into the world of fairy tales, and invites us to try to navigate this world. But we know too much and as that world changes us, we change it.

We know that in the real world a wedding is not the end of the story, that it is not a guarantee of happiness. Going into the fairy tale woods with the knowledge we have will shape that world into something very different. We know that the people who claim to be doing good, aren't always. A child might accept the idea that killing a giant is unambiguously good. But we live in a world with war, abortion, mercy killing, and capital punishment. Killing suddenly isn't all that clear-cut. Some people would say killing is never good. Others will point out that killing is sanctioned in the Bible. Which are we to believe? There are no easy answers.

Into the Woods is a very special show. In Act I, we are presented with a (relatively) conventional fairy tale that ends with a Happily Ever After. But in Act II, that world of black and white is dissected, deconstructed, examined more closely. We see that getting our Happily Ever After, getting what we want sometimes necessitates acts we may not be proud of, acts that have unforeseen consequences down the road. When we go into these woods, we bring our adult world with us, where people sometimes lie and steal.

We've already learned all those lessons about honesty, bravery, and obedience (though we may not always practice them). *Into the Woods* teaches us lessons—things some of us adults have not yet learned—about consequences, about responsibility to the community. (Maybe Clinton needs to see this show.) "No One is Alone" isn't just a song that promises support in our time of need; it's also a song that cautions us to be aware of how our actions affect others, reminding us that we do not live in a vacuum. One line says, "Careful—no one is alone." It's this "careful" that raises this show out of the ordinary.

Some people have criticized *Into the Woods* for being too preachy, for spelling out its lessons too completely. Real fairy tales never explicitly state their morals, leaving that work for the child to do. But this is a fairy tale for adults, and, as we all know, adults are far less perceptive than children.

REMEMBERING INTO THE WOODS

I loved doing this show. Absolute fun. I was nervous about singing, as the only singing I had really done was karaoke, but the company and environment were so incredible that I felt at home. I remember Justin and I had the arduous task of transforming Karl from the Wolf into Cinderella's Prince. This entailed starting backstage, stripping him of the Wolf vest, racing upstairs, wiping away sweat and make-up, running through St Marcus' Church, helping him into Prince clothes, and then downstairs for his cue to enter behind the audience. Thanks, Scott. Great idea. Luckily we made it every night. During the run of the show, I developed a wonderful bruise on my left shin and scars on both wrists from falling. It wasn't so much falling as slamming myself into a wooden riser. The audience reaction was more than worth it, especially one night, when an older couple gasped "Oh dear! I hope he's all right!"

—Sean Pritchett, "Rapunzel's Prince"

The show was *Into the Woods*. I was Cinderella's Dead Mother, the Giant, and Granny. The cast did a lot of marching through the audience. Lots of bobbing and weaving—single file, so as not to run into each other. I was Granny at the time of The Incident. All I remember is two Princes coming at me at the same time. I tried to "weave" out of the way, but in my struggle to remember those damn Sondheim lyrics, I had forgotten about the ramps which extended out from the stage. Yes, I avoided the Princes, but not the ramps. My feet were caught under the ramp and down I went. I believe St. Louis experienced a 5.3 on the Richter scale that evening. I managed to get myself up and march through the audience, singing and smiling. Instantly, my feet were growing. I decided not to take off my character shoes, believing I would never get them back on. My feet were the feet of the Giant. They became a lovely color of purple. Not to be one to complain or miss a party, I went out after the show with the cast, with the help of Vicadin and a couple of Bud Lights. Later, the x-rays showed I had fractured my feet in 3 places. The irony is that I was given many compliments later in the run regarding the 'cute' way Granny was walking because of my injury. And so as the old adage goes—the show must go on.
—Mo Monahan, "Granny, Giant's Wife, Cinderella's Mother"

I'm one of those people who starts laughing when things get tense. Or when someone falls. So I got a good laugh the night Mo Monahan fell in a heap during the show in her Granny clothes. Unfortunately, I didn't actually get to see the fall (so I don't have the rights to re-enact it), but I got to witness the aftermath. I found Mo sitting in the bathroom, moaning and actually crying some. Now, of course that's not funny, but I couldn't control my laughter when she explained what was wrong. Here's the direct quote: "I fell…I fell out there…I fell flat on my face…in front of all those people, I tripped and fell…flat on my stupid face!" And while I certainly cared that Mo had hurt herself, I nearly gnawed the inside of my cheek raw trying to keep from cackling loudly, as the show was still in progress. Needless to say, Mo spent the remainder of the run wearing a walking cast on her ankle.

—Beck Hunter, "Cinderella's Stepmother"

New Line's production of *Into The Woods* had a beautiful set, an extremely talented cast, superb and imaginative direction, a very good band, a masterful score and script, and an anatomically complete Wolf. Karl, who played the Wolf, would dance and move around the audience area (Scott blocked the show using the entire theatre as a stage) during rehearsals in a very provocative way. He would slither and slink and use pelvic thrusts that we knew would be in audience members' faces. The Wolf's costume was to have a suggestive bulge in the crotch area and everyone thought the pelvic thrusts would be fun for the audience. When the Wolf's costume was delivered, the bulge was more than a suggestion. It was unmistakable proof of the Wolf's gender. Needless to say, the pelvic thrusts took on a whole new dynamic. The script didn't give us any clues about the Wolf's first name, but if I were to venture a guess, I think it would be Dick.

—Steve Johnson, "Narrator/Mysterious Man"

I loved playing Rapunzel and having long blonde hair. Being of Asian descent, I had never pictured myself as a blonde. I even bleached my eyebrows to be more blonde! What I really enjoyed more than anything about *Into the Woods* was the environment. The entire theatre was transformed into the woods, and the stage incorporated hills and life-sized trees that came alive! It was a spectacular set, and you couldn't help feeling like you were somewhere else, somewhere where giants lurk, witches live, and the big bad wolf could jump out from anywhere. I have to mention a funny-in-an-odd-sort-of-way thing. One time, when I was trying to ask the costume designer a question, her response (with English accent) as she went by was, "You're not to speak to me while I'm walking!" I could hardly believe my ears! Now I love to tell that story, and you have to laugh.

—Kimi Short, "Rapunzel"

All of us girls were crammed into the rear dressing room of the St. Marcus, a room so cluttered and full of bugs, dead and alive, that I refused to take off my shoes unless I was standing on the towel I brought. Beck told me one night that if she were to die young in some freak accident, she wanted me to create a memorial fund for her which would rehab and redecorate the St. Marcus dressing rooms. As New Line is no longer performing at the St. Marcus Theatre, I'm now glad on two counts that Beck is still alive.

—Johanna Schloss, "Lucinda"

Out of Line Productions Presents

Head Games

◆

a world premiere
Written and Directed by Scott Miller
August 5–28, 1999
St. Marcus Theatre, St. Louis

THE CAST
Eddie—Sean Pritchett
Grace—Sarah Laak
Michael—Michael A. Naggi
Chaz—Justin Heinrich
Danny—Michael Deak
Tucker—Michael Bowdern
Willy—Bradley Calise

THE ARTISTIC STAFF
Director—Scott Miller
Set & Costume Designer—Justin Heinrich
Lighting Designer—Tim Lord
Lighting Technician—Amy Francis Schott
Stage Manager—Rebecca Hunter
Box Office Manager—Steve Dohrmann
Massage Consultant—Chris Brenner
Graphic Design—Zachary Lips
Photography—Robert Stevens

THE REVIEWS

"Miller provides an intelligent and interesting context, genuinely witty and clever lines, and a wholesomeness and honesty both unexpected—under the circumstances—and exhilarating...This, besides the verbal brilliance, is where Miller takes *Head Games* well beyond the dick-play genre. His director's program note and the piece in last week's *RFT* tell the audience in advance what Miller is going to do, but it's like a magician's explaining a trick before he performs it and still amazing his spectators."—Harry Weber, *The Riverfront Times*

"The funniest moment in *Head Games* occurs when a character questions the artistic integrity of a director who plans to stage a play with gratuitous nudity. The irony is that the actor expressing these sentiments is gratuitously nude...Miller is an astute critic, and these questions are obviously important to him...The arguments about theater and sexuality are thought-provoking, balanced and often amusing."—Gerry Kowarsky, *St. Louis Post-Dispatch*

AUTHOR'S NOTES

Last summer, two things happened at once. First, New Line Theatre found itself with a minor debt as our regular season of musical theatre was closing. Second, while I was online one day, I ran into David Dillon, the author of *Party*, a gay stage comedy with full frontal nudity. *Party* had been a huge hit in Chicago, then went to off-Broadway and other cities around the U.S. When Dillon found out I ran a theatre company, he suggested we produce his play. I told him New Line only did issue-oriented musical theatre, but later, I couldn't stop thinking about the profits his play would probably earn, easily wiping out our deficit. After some debate, we decided to create an offshoot company, Out of Line Productions, to produce *Party*. And it made pots of money.

This summer, finding ourselves in another financial crunch, my thoughts again turned toward a gay comedy with nudity to fill our coffers. I went in search of a play to match *Party* in its wit, its intelligence, and its warmth, but could find nothing. On a lark, I started writing my own. (I had written eight musicals, but no plays.) What I ended up with was a gay comedy called *Head Games*, a play that addressed the growing genre of gay comedies with nudity, sometimes referred to as "dick plays." The characters in my play debated the use of nudity and obscenity on stage, the question of what "gay theatre" is or should be, America's preoccupation with and fear of sexuality, the decision of an artistically "pure" theatre company to do a blatantly commercial work, and other issues. *Head Games* became not only a "dick play" itself, but also a commentary on and deconstruction of "dick plays."

The first act of *Head Games* is a debate on whether or not plays like *Head Games* should exist and whether or not they are art, with the characters voicing every objection I heard when New Line first produced *Party*. The second act of *Head Games* redefines the first act, actually becoming the "dick play" that the first act describes, suggesting finally that all the furor is really over nothing more than depicting events and conversations which are (or could be) a part of real life. And isn't that what theatre is about—making sense of the world, making order out of the chaos of our lives? And laughing at ourselves?

It will be interesting to see how you react to *Head Games*. Not only does it poke fun at me, at New Line, and at itself, it also pokes fun at the audiences who come to see it. Like Oliver Stone's *Natural Born Killers*, Wes Craven's *Scream*, and Bob Fosse's stage musical *Chicago*, *Head Games* takes the form of that which it criticizes.

And it has a lot of fun in the process.

REMEMBERING HEAD GAMES

My second show with New Line firmly cemented this company into my heart. *Head Games* was a blast and there was never a dull moment. I was never nervous about performing naked. I saw it as a costume. I even stopped playing rugby during the run, to prevent damage. That said, however, it didn't help that the stage was cold from the AC, when Sarah and my naked self opened the show each night. I'd do anything I could to get the blood flowing and loosen things up before entering. Some nights it worked. Luckily, by the end of the show, things were warmer and I could withdraw with some pride. In rehearsal a running gag put me in stitches. Miguel, as Tucker, would leave the stage for the toilet. Though never saying anything, if you looked closely, he took a magazine. It was something so subtle, so simple and so absurdly honest that it would get me going every time. During the run, I'd be backstage waiting to see which one he had brought.

—Sean Pritchett, "Eddie"

Head Games was a real lesson in writing a show. I kind of stumbled into the act of writing it to begin with, and my first draft was only twenty-five pages long. We sat down and read it out loud and everyone agreed it was worth continuing. So I kept writing, kept expanding things, clarifying things, connecting things, trying to keep the jokes coming even when the topics turned serious, as they did frequently throughout the show. After all, the show was (partly) about what gay theatre should be, whether or not it should even exist, whether or not nudity prevents a show from being serious theatre, and whether even "legitimate" motivation can truly legitimize actors taking their clothes off onstage. As with all the shows I've written, lots of rewrites were done during rehearsals, and the actors were wonderful about being gentle when something didn't work and helpful when I was stuck for an idea. But the roughest part was the ending. The second-to-last scene ended with high energy and a big punch line. Then there was a short five-minute final scene that tied up all the loose ends and resolved the plot. But we found that though audiences were screaming with laughter after that second-to-last scene, the response to the final scene was always tepid. We tried to speed up the scene change. We tried lots of things. Then I decided to cut that last scene. The show worked ten times better.

But I knew that there were quite a few loose ends, that the ending was now unsatisfying dramatically. It really bothered me but the audience had spoken. So we left the last scene off for the rest of the run. It wasn't until the show was produced in Los Angeles (very badly—don't ask) that I finally figured out how to combine those last two scenes.

—Scott Miller, playwright and director

A New Line Songbook

♦

a world premiere
Featuring songs from past New Line shows, including
Attempting the Absurd, Breaking Out in Harmony, Assassins, Pippin, In the Blood, Company, Sweeney Todd, Passion, Jacques Brel, The Ballad of Little Mikey, March of the Falsettos, Songs for a New World, Camelot, Into the Woods, and other shows
Conceived by Scott Miller
October 9, 1999
St. Marcus Theatre, St. Louis

THE CAST
Karl Berberich, Kevin Collier, Cindy Duggan, Keith Hale, Alison Helmer, Rebecca Hunter, Lisa Karpowicz, Keith Price, Angie (Shultz) Reinert, John Rhine, Dan Sattel, Deborah Sharn, Kimi Short, Steven R. Johnson

THE ARTISTIC STAFF
Director—Scott Miller
Lighting Designer—Amy Francis Schott

Floyd Collins

♦

a St. Louis premiere
Music and Lyrics by Adam Guettel
Book and Additional Lyrics by Tina Landau
November 4-20, 1999
St. Marcus Theatre, St. Louis

THE CAST
Floyd Collins—Troy Schnider
Homer Collins—Eric Whitman
Nellie Collins—Kimi Short
Lee Collins—Steven R. Johnson
Jane Collins—Mary "Mo" Monahan
William "Skeets" Miller—Dan Sattel
Bee Doyle—Karl Berberich
Ed Bishop—Michael Deak
Jewel Estes—Colin DeVaughan
H.T. Carmichael—Patrick Kerwin
Cliff Roney/Reporter—Chris Brenner
Dr. Hazlett/Reporter—Keith Hale
Reporter—John Rhine

THE ARTISTIC STAFF
Directors—Scott Miler and Alison Helmer
Assistant Director—Kevin Corlett

Lighting Designer—Mark Schilling
Costume Designer—Elizabeth Krausnick
Set Designer and Scene Painter—Karl Berberich
Set Construction Assistant—Adam Lewis
Stage Manager—Amy Francis Schott
Sound Technician—Chris Clark
Box Office Manager—Steve Dohrmann
Graphic Designer—Tracy Collins

THE BAND
Piano—Neal Richardson
Violin—Bill Bauer
Guitar/Banjo—Kathy Schottel
Percussion—Adam Kopff

THE REVIEWS

"New Line Theatre…continues the hot streak that began last season with *Camelot* and *Into the Woods*. Scott Miller's productions always are small in scale, but the imaginative scope of these recent shows has impressive depth…It offers perspective instead of self-indulgence, imagination instead of ego. It's a compelling musical and one that is well-suited to the New Line Theatre's stripped-down style."—Judith Newmark, *St. Louis-Post Dispatch*

"Adam Guettel, the composer and lyricist, and Tina Landau have turned this dark, sad tale into a remarkable piece of musical theater that, although hardly flawless, is consistently interesting both in its music and in the way the story is told…New Line Theatre has fielded a strong cast whose vocal abilities are generally matches for Guettel's often demanding music…and what a pleasure it was to hear natural, unamplified voices."—Harry Weber, *The Riverfront Times*

"Scott Miller's New Line Theatre company, in the small cave of the St. Marcus Theatre, is shouting out a beautiful exploratory cave call: they have been delving into the subterranean recesses of musical theatre for some years, and now they've opened a fine production that epitomizes their own search...The cast abounds with strong performances."—Steve Callahan, KDHX-FM

DIRECTOR'S NOTES

Raucous comedy. Great tenderness. Muscular, powerful music. Simple folk ballads. Family, faith, metaphysics. It's all there in *Floyd Collins*, one of the most spectacular first efforts in the history of musical theatre.

The critics have gone wild over this show. *New York Newsday* called it "one of the three or four truly great music theatre scores of the last decade." *Entertainment Weekly* said, "The melodies soar...In Adam Guettel a vital new musical theatre writer has emerged." *New York Magazine* said, "This is the original and daring musical of our day..., a powerhouse." *Variety* said it was "easy to admire..., sometimes ravishing." *The San Diego Union Tribune* called it "a daring and original piece of musical theater." *The Los Angeles Times* called it "plaintive, often inspired...Adam Guettel is a composer for the new century."

With *Floyd Collins*, composer-lyricist Adam Guettel (rhymes with *kettle*) has clearly established himself as the most likely candidate to lead the next generation into the musical theatre terrain that Stephen Sondheim has explored for the last forty years. Floyd Collins is a musical full of a complexity and sophistication worthy of Sondheim, yet also full of the emotional force that this story demands; because, though it is a story about media exploitation, greed, glory, and prejudice, at its core, it is even more about family and faith. It is one of those musicals, like *West Side Story, Company,* and *Ragtime,* which could only have been written by Americans. There is a brashness, an openness, and a muscularity in *Floyd Collins* that is uniquely American.

Guettel and his bookwriter Tina Landau have tackled a most unlikely subject for a musical. Most of the story takes place after Floyd has been trapped a hundred feet underground. How do you make a musical about a character who can't move? The answer is twofold. First, they realized the most compelling story here is an internal one; the almost supernatural connection between Floyd and Nellie, the powerful brotherly bond between Floyd and Homer, Floyd's indomitably American spirit, and his blind optimism in the face of incredible obstacles. Second, Guettel separated the two worlds—above ground and underground—by giving them each their own sound. Above ground, the music is an only slightly altered bluegrass Kentucky folk sound; rollicking, simple, honest. Below the surface is Floyd's world, and it has its own music. Here is where Guettel uses the sophisticated, complex sounds that owe something to the work of Stephen Sondheim; full of soaring, gorgeous melodies; unusual, quirky rhythms; and fascinating, interconnected musical themes that weave together to create a beautiful musical tapestry.

Guettel and Landau have written a musical about a real American hero, still today considered the greatest cave explorer in American history. And they've done it with such care and such skill that it ends up being one of the greatest musicals you'll ever see. We just hope we've done this magnificent work justice.

REMEMBERING FLOYD COLLINS

Several years after college I found myself far from the theatre, doing graphic design in a retail music store, when one of my coworkers, a former university music instructor, got a call from a local theatre company desperate to replace the lead in an upcoming production of *Brigadoon*. Aware of my background, he gave them my name; two weeks later I was performing my first role since college. That was the spark. Three more lead roles built my confidence enough that I sought out professional theatre companies, not for the money, but for the challenge. I was tired of being a big fish in a little pond, but the old fears returned. Was I good enough? I had to give it a shot, and another local actor suggested New Line Theatre. I knew nothing about them, but I trusted him and soon learned they were about to hold auditions for *Floyd Collins*. In my wildest dreams I never imagined a St. Louis company would take on a show this personal and this excruciatingly difficult. I clearly remember my only request on the audition form: "I just want to sing." They cast me as Floyd, and, along with music director Neal Richardson, pushed me harder and farther than I ever dreamed. To this day I'm still shocked they had the guts to take on a show like this, but you have to realize New Line does it time and again over and over. Scott simply does what inspires him. It's truly remarkable. The fact that he's willing to cast someone he's never seen before, and has the wherewithal to pull it off, astounds me. So, do I have what it takes? Who knows, that's for others to decide, but I'll never stop seeking out challenges and working hard. I have New Line Theatre to thank for this outlook, and *Floyd Collins* and many future productions to look forward to because of it.

—Troy Schnider, "Floyd Collins"

For me, the most wonderful moment of doing this show was standing backstage late in the second act while Floyd sings his last song and realizes he's going to die in the cave. For me, that was the emotional high point. When Troy would sing the line: "Will my mama be there waiting for me?" I would get shivers and have a huge lump in my throat the whole time I was saying my closing monologue. *Floyd Collins* was far and away the most touching show I've ever experienced. I will always cherish the memory.

—Dan Sattel, "Skeets Miller"

During the rehearsal process for *Floyd Collins*, Scott did a tremendous amount of research about this true story. In fact, Scott, Alison, Troy, and Amy traveled to Kentucky and saw the actual area where the show is set. They even brought back pictures and souvenirs of their trek to Floyd country. All of this reminded the cast that our characters were real people, and we got to know them a little better. But the biggest reminder happened on opening night. A group of actual cavers attended and sat in the front row with their cave helmets on. We thought that was kind of a strange thing to do and were poking fun at them backstage. During intermission, Scott talked to these folks and found out how much of a folk hero Floyd Collins is to cavers everywhere, even seventy-five years after his death. In a sense, it was like having friends of Floyd in the audience. That was pretty cool. Oh yeah, the cavers liked the show.

—Steve Johnson, "Lee Collins"

I never want to yodel again in my life. I don't think Scott would ever be happy with music that was simple and easy. And because of this, I don't think his performers would either. I have wanted to try other theater groups, but I don't. I keep thinking, "But they won't be like New Line's shows." I believe in what Scott does and the education in theater that he has given me. Also [I'm thankful] for the wonderful opportunities for personal growth and growth as a performer. I can never be grateful enough for all the true friendships I have made through New Line. I am proud to say that I am a part of New Line and will always be. Thank you Scott Miller.

—Chris Brenner, "Cliff Roney, Yodeler"

It was in the fall of 1999. *Floyd* was upon us and I took the job as set designer. I tried different ideas. In a small theatre like St. Marcus, there isn't much room for anything extensive. So I had to wing it. I needed this unit set to be a cave, a forest, a gathering area. I knew it would get done. I just couldn't calculate how well. I was in a bit of a panic. I needed to catch a vacation. I needed to really focus. I took a trip to Springfield. I knew how the set would be built, but the detail was crucial. That first night in Springfield was to be the time of clarity. I lay on my back on my friend's floor (a bit sauced), watching a candle flicker light on the ceiling. I felt something on my side. I look down to my chest, and in the little light that was in the room, I noticed two long antennae sweeping the air. I froze. "I hate cockroaches," I thought. All the lights go on and my friend is grabbing a shoe to kill this bug. In a flash, I realized what was on me...a cricket! I shouted, "No! Don't kill it!" Floyd talked to crickets! It jumped off of me and disappeared into the house. In the instant I saw that cricket, I saw the detail of the set. In my head it was complete (crazy, huh?). That was a great spiritual moment for me. I believe in many Eastern beliefs and one belief is that crickets are fortune tellers, prognosticators. I had a moment of connection with something else, somewhere else. And the energy used me to create the right set. It turned out to be one of my favorite works of art to date. (Thank you, Mark, for the perfect lighting.) *Floyd* and my time doing that show really helped me deal with problems I had been struggling with, [helped me] shine in the face of adversity.

—Karl Berberich, set designer, "Bee Doyle"

During rehearsals for *Floyd Collins*, Troy, Alison, and I drove to Kentucky to see Floyd's cave. The lady at the Floyd Collins Museum told us where the cave was in which Floyd had been trapped. We drove down the road and found a small sign by the side that said "Sand Cave." There were no arrows, no map, no directions. We started down the dirt path, and after a few wrong turns, we finally found it—Floyd Collins' Sand Cave, where Floyd was trapped and died, where people had argued over rescue theories, where thousands of gawkers and onlookers had assembled seventy-four years before. We found the tiny passage through which Floyd had squeezed. It was utterly magical and emotionally overwhelming. I felt like I was about to cry. I couldn't believe we were there. It was the feeling you get standing in a beautiful cathedral. We then drove up the road further to find Floyd's grave, and an elderly couple who had been driving by stopped when they saw us in the graveyard.

The man had been a cave guide many years before and had carried Floyd's coffin when they had moved it to that cemetery. They told us so many great stories and then told us how to find the unmarked Crystal Cave, which Floyd had opened to the public before his death in 1925. The next day, we found the small dirt road they had described, behind a locked gate. We parked and walked several miles down this road, not knowing for sure if it was even the right road. We found a couple buildings which we thought might be a house and a ticket office Floyd had built. While Alison and Troy took pictures, I found a path and ventured down it. I came across homemade stairs and a railing leading down to an entrance into a hill. I had found Crystal Cave and I screamed myself hoarse running back up to them. The entrance was sealed behind a big iron door, but when Troy pushed on the door, it opened, and to our great surprise we were able to walk inside the first chamber of Floyd's cave, to stand on the floor he had smoothed, to breathe the air he had once breathed. It was an experience I'll never forget.

—Scott Miller, director

What I remember most about the show is reuniting with Scott, and working with him for the first time in years. Whenever I've worked with Scott, it's always been an educational experience for me because he is so knowledgeable about the material he covers for any show he does. This was the first musical I had done since I graduated college. Since then I have concentrated mostly on music-writing, singing, and acting from time to time in various film and TV projects. So this was a welcome change of pace for me, as well as a sort of homecoming, since the musical stage is my first love. I remember everyone involved in *Floyd Collins* being a bit overwhelmed at first by the complexity of the material. Not just the score, but the story behind it too. This show is also a fine example of the type of material that Scott chooses for New Line, and why I believe the company has survived, and will thrive in the many years to come. New Line's productions do more than entertain people like other theatre companies or shows, where you leave the theatre afterwards, and within fifteen minutes forget what you just saw. New Line challenges the audience, and gives the audience something to think about after they leave the theatre. I'm not familiar with many other theatre companies, besides perhaps the Steppenwolf Theatre Company in Chicago, that sets the bar so high in the choosing and executing of material, whether it's a popular classic, a lesser known piece, or a world premiere of an original work; where the result is a growing and learning experience for the artists onstage and behind the scenes as well as quality entertainment for the audience. Here's to ten—and hopefully many more—years for New Line! I hope that I'm lucky enough to be a part of your process again and again in the future.

—Eric Whitman, "Homer"

The Ballad of Floyd Collins—A Parody
(To the tune of theme song for *The Beverly Hillbillies*, with parody lyrics by Scott Miller.)

Come and listen to a show about a man named Floyd,
So damn weird that you'll prob'ly get annoyed,
All about Kentucky and a fella in a cave—
Not so very happy but it surely is brave.
   (spoken)
Brave theatre. Dissonant music. Hard to understand.

At the openin' of the show, this Floyd goes down,
Crawling on the stage, kinda squirmin' all around,
First ten minutes, he gets trapped real tight,
And he doesn't move a muscle for the rest of the night.
   (spoken)
Long night. Just sits there. No choreography.

And that's about the size of it, the whole friggin' show,
All in all, about as fun as choppin' off your toe.
Lots of heavy drama and some really long songs,
A-weepin' and a-wailin' where the comedy belongs.
  (spoken)
Just a joke or two. That's all we ask.

Now, the first thing you know, they'll be doing it agin,
Another damn musical about a mortal sin,
More crazy melodies a-dancin' in your head,
And sure, by the end, well, the hero will be dead.
  (spoken)
Stone dead. Depressing as hell…

Out on Broadway 2000

◆

a world premiere sequel
Featuring songs from *Rent, Yentl, Fiddler on the Roof, Working, Grease, Little Shop of Horrors, Annie Get Your Gun, Guys and Dolls, Ballroom, Aspects of Love, Faust, Cabaret, South Pacific, Jesus Christ Superstar, Closer Than Ever, Woman of the Year, Follies, Ragtime, A New Brain*, and other shows
Conceived by Scott Miller
March 9-April 1, 2000
St. Marcus Theatre, St. Louis

THE CAST
Chris Brenner, Tracy Collins, Robb Kennedy, Keith Thompson, Eddie Webb

THE ARTISTIC STAFF
Director—Scott Miller
Lighting Designer—Amy Francis Schott
Costume Consultant—Tim Kent
Box Office Manager—Steve Dohrmann
Graphic Designer—Tracy Collins
Pianist—Scott Miller

THE REVIEWS

"At least the quirky little [St. Marcus] theater is going out in style. Scott Miller's revue, which presents musical theater songs in a gay context, has graceful, small-scale proportions, just right for this theater in terms of music, voice and staging. Furthermore, the show's message—a plea for tolerance, particularly in regard to sexual orientation—is a fair summation of the point that many St. Marcus shows have made...Miller even works in "Danny Boy." But the ensemble rendition changes the terms so drastically that "Danny Boy" gains fresh meaning, tender and powerful. The song underscores the value of shows like this one: They reveal the familiar in a fresh light. Audiences need places that offer us that perspective."—Judith Newmark, *St. Louis Post-Dispatch*

"*Out on Broadway 2000*, Scott Miller's beguiling assemblage of show tunes, looks like a lot of fun to do...This show makes you want to dish about the wise and witty performances of each singer."—Sally Cragin, *The Riverfront Times*

"The gimmick sometimes works too, culling surprises from familiar lyrics when placed in a new context. I discovered I'd never really listened to the lyrics of 'Far From the Home I Love,' from *Fiddler on the Roof*, until I heard it in *Out on Broadway 2000*."—Bob Wilcox, KDHX-FM

"New Line Theatre's *Out on Broadway 2000* gender-reversed Broadway and cabaret standards and provided dreamy entertainment. All that was missing was the clink of ice cubes and a blue haze of cigarette smoke."—*The Riverfront Times*, "Best of 2000"

DIRECTOR'S NOTES

When we put together the first *Out on Broadway* in March 1996, we had no idea that there would be such enormous public demand for more performances that we'd have to bring it back in August of that same year. We never thought there'd be a cast album. And we certainly never thought we'd be doing a sequel four years later.

But here we are.

So much has changed since 1996. *Will and Grace* is on television every week, getting great ratings, and three more shows with gay lead characters are planned for next season. And for good or bad, gay Americans are every bit as visible as straight Americans on Jerry Springer and the other talk shows.

Gay marriage has become one of the top issues in the country, with the Vermont Supreme Court ordering the state legislature to give gay couples equal rights, with Californians voting on a referendum against equal marriage rights for gay couples on March 7, and with the Hawaii gay marriage case still rumbling despite setbacks. In contrast, a study just released says 2.5 million gay Americans are currently in heterosexual marriages.

The issue of adoption for gay couples is coming before courts around the country. Anti-gay discrimination in groups like the Boy Scouts is being actively challenged in the courts, and in some cases, is being condemned.

As the presidential races heat up, gay issues are on the agenda everywhere you look. Both Al Gore and Bill Bradley are actively courting gay voters. And even the most conservative Republicans are being forced to acknowledge us and address our issues.

And yet, Matthew Shepard was brutally murdered in Wyoming just for being gay. Billy Jack Gaither was murdered in Georgia for the same reason. And they're not the only ones.

One of the purposes of the original *Out on Broadway* was to tell gay teens and closeted gay men and women that it's okay to be gay, that they can be gay and still be proud of who they are, that being gay is not a sickness. With all the increased visibility for gay Americans, perhaps that's not as necessary today as it was four years ago.

The other purpose of the original show was to demonstrate how alike gay and straight people are, and how alike gay and straight love is.

That is still necessary because, even though we are all alike deep down, the world still does not treat us alike. It's amazing how easy it was for most of these songs, originally written for straight characters, to work in a gay context—but they do, precisely because gay people think and feel most of the same things as their straight friends and families. And that message can't be spread far enough or fast enough.

So enjoy the show. Laugh along with us, cry along with us, but most importantly, remember that we are your brothers and sisters, parents, friends, neighbors, and co-workers. Remember that many of us want to marry. Some of us want to have kids. And all of us want the respect we deserve.

*H*air

Book and Lyrics by Gerome Ragni and James Rado
Music by Galt MacDermot
June 8-July 1, 2000
A.E. Hotchner Drama Studio
Washington University, St. Louis

THE OSAGE TRIBE
David Aikman, Kiné Brown, Bradley Calise, Karl Brian Clark, Alexis D
.Coleman, Ken Haller, Justin Heinrich, Beck Hunter, Robin Kelso,
Terry L. Love, Mo Monahan, Uchenna Ogu, John Rhine, John Sparger,
Nicole Trueman

THE ARTISTIC STAFF
Director/Music Director—Scott Miller
Lighting Designer—Paul Summers
Costume Designers—Justin Heinrich & Bradley Calise
Set Designer & Scene Painter—Karl Berberich
Set Construction Assistant—Adam Lewis
Stage Manager—Amy Francis Schott
Box Office Manager—Steve Dohrmann

THE BAND
Piano/Conductor—Scott Miller
Lead Guitar—Dale Hampton

Rhythm Guitar—M. Joshua Ryan
Bass—Darin Johnson
Trumpet—Paul Hooper
Percussion—Adam Kopff

THE REVIEWS

"A gripping production from New Line Theatre...The in-the-round presentation, with actors running through the audience, suits director Scott Miller's intense style. His production moves with the studied emotional focus of a dream—or a memory...And this production perfectly captures the deep, genuine anger that the Vietnam War provoked at home. 'Three-Five-Zero-Zero,' a song in which the hallucinating Claude envisions his hippie friends falling in battle, is a stunning depiction of how immediate the threat felt to people a world away from the war."—Judith Newmark, *St. Louis Post-Dispatch*

"New Line Theatre's production of *Hair*, which opened last weekend in the A.E. Hotchner Drama Studio on the Washington University campus, may pull you into a gallop down memory lane (if you're older) or (if you're younger) may cause an attack of envy because your parents lived in much more interesting times than you do. Whatever the effect, a strong, musical cast make the book, music and lyrics seem as fresh and fun as they were in 1968."—Harry Weber, *The Riverfront Times*

"At once historical and iconoclastic, this classic hippie postcard from the summer of love remains as brittle and quirky as ever, but the New Line production reveled in the shaggy spirit, and proved largely enjoyable."—Brian McCary, KDHX-FM

DIRECTOR'S NOTES

It is 1968 and the youth of America are lost.
Their parents, still celebrating the prosperity that followed World War II, have raised social drinking to an art form; they are bathing in

the excesses of capitalistic materialism; and they are showering their children with everything anyone could want—except the nourishment of the soul.

These young people have all the physical trappings of happiness but don't know who they are, where they belong, what is expected of them. More of them are going to college than ever before, where they learn to think independently, to question the status quo, and to reject their parents' long-held, arbitrary definitions of morality, success, and happiness. These young people see racism run rampant in America, with lynchings still common in the South. They see American youths shipped off to southeast Asia to fight a war which has nothing to do with America and which appears to be unjust, immoral, racist, and impossible to win. They see disregard for the environment in the unchecked progress of American industry. And they see a culture that now worships at the feet of a new God—consumerism.

What do these kids want? They want to erase all the rules and start over, creating a new society that makes sense; one built on the idea of celebrating all the wonderful, magical, indefinable things that make us human; the things that unite us; the things that join us to the rest of the natural world. They ask why we have such restrictive rules of sexuality. Is it because some culture from long ago wanted to control inheritance? Or was it about the perpetuating of a particular ethnic group? Why do we have such restrictive rules about drugs? Is it because once we taste the liberation of mind-expanding substances, we'll be harder to control? Why do the adults who drink like fishes at cocktail parties so self-righteously condemn marijuana? Why do they so strongly condemn all drugs, when so many other cultures highly value the ritual use of hallucinogenic drugs to achieve a higher level of consciousness and to find God? Why do so many people call themselves people of faith but act in such immoral ways?

Our tribe has not come to insult you or the values you hold dear. Our intention is not to shock or upset—though we may do that too. We have come to celebrate our humanness, the joy of living, our connection to each other and to the world around us, our God-given sexuality, and the wonders and mysteries of the human mind and body.

We have come to ask you to join us in rejecting violence, hatred, fear, and judgement wherever we find it, to question the way things have always been, to look at the world with a fresh eye, and to resolve to change the things that need changing.

Especially here and now, in the year 2000, an election year, consider whether we need more guns in the world, whether we value our children enough, whether we value our freedom enough, whether we value our planet enough, and whether people should be discriminated against because of the way they look or who they fall in love with.

It is a new age. Everything is ready. It's time to change the world.

REMEMBERING HAIR

Hair was the first show I have ever done where I really felt as though I was saying something important; and, perhaps even more importantly, it was the first show I have done where I really believed in what I was saying. Though the show is over thirty years old, any criticisms about the show being "dated" have never held much weight with me. While the main conflict (Vietnam) is no longer being fought, the scars of that war live on to this day, just as many of the other issues in the show do (racism, acceptance of those different from you, the ridiculous and arbitrary way society stigmatizes all recreational drugs). As I became more and more involved in the show, everything we were fighting for in the show became more important to me, and I actually began to understand how it must have felt when people began reaching out to one another in the sixties, with the hopes that they would actually make the world a better place.

—Bradley Calise, "Margaret Mead"

My relationship with Miller began just over ten years ago. I was a bright-eyed, clean shaven optimist a year out of college who thought, after one too many drinks most likely, I was to be an actor. Miller cast me in my first St. Louis show, *Deathtrap*, a play he was producing for another company while finding his way with New Line. It was only my second show, but he gave me a shot as the manipulative Clifford, and my acting career was on its way.

The next seven years snaked me from local to regional stages, to national tours, and finally landed me in L.A. for a spell struggling in film and television and honing my extracurricular skills. I retired from acting at the ripe old age of thirty and moved back to St. Louis. And there I found a thriving theatre community with New Line as one of the major players.

Chances are I would've stayed from the footlights, happily grinding the stone at a warehouse, had it not been for an audition notice in the *RFT*—*HAIR*, the Tribal Love Rock Musical from the late '60s to be produced by New Line and directed by Miller. A show I had always wanted to perform, but never had the opportunity. I couldn't pass on at least auditioning.

Whether Miller had been drinking or smoking too much on the evening of his final casting, he graced me with the role of Berger—a decision that will forever bond me in his creative and artistic debt. A role that enabled me to exorcise some demons within. A show so powerful as to compress yet amplify scores of emotions for those who experience it.

Hair is a show in which the Whole is certainly nothing without its Parts, but also where the Parts are nothing unto themselves until summed. Yes, we all know "Aquarius" and the title song "Hair," and most of us recognize "Easy to be Hard." But the book itself is a series of mostly non-linear non-sequitors strung out in a drug-induced mélange thinly plotted against the political and cultural climate of the times. Or is it?

The rehearsal process was none as I had ever encountered. At times frightening—at others liberating. The story line was confusing; the characters sporadic. A lead role was changed with less than a week before curtain. I admit I was unsure of how the final outcome would translate, but my faith in Miller never waned. On final dress, everything made sense. The power of the music and the message of the show, under the eccentric guidance of Miller, came searing through in synaptic waves. We all felt it. We all got it.

Nearly every night after rehearsal, a small group would get together for drinks and eats. I thought it important for the Tribe to bond offstage as well as on. And although the participants shifted from night to night, Miller and I were steadfast. This gave us a wonderful opportunity, outside of rehearsals, to discuss and dissect not only the show, but a multitude of topics relating in large and small or none at all ways. And through this discovery and revelatory process, Miller was able to instill acceptance and trust and fuel me to portray what I hope was a truthful performance.

As for the show itself, he brought out the passion and power that it truly possesses. He dug to the core and revealed the moral meaning behind it all. Propelled by an improvisationally talented group of musicians, a subtle yet dramatic lighting design and the freedom of a skeletal set, Miller brought *Hair* to life and drove it marching and protesting into the hearts/minds/souls of those in the seats. And as with all the pieces I've seen New Line produce and Miller direct, he gave audiences the Truth. Not one person who experienced this show, be him spectator or performer, walked away unaffected.

Did I experience change? Certainly. Will I perform again? Hard to say. But *Hair* definitely puts a helluva capper on a spotty, sporadic decade of performing. I am emphatically proud of that show and am honored to have been a part of it.

And although New Line revived the show the following summer, there were changes in my life that made me unable to get on the bus. A month after we closed *Hair*, I became a father. Unfortunately, the geographical location of my baby boy, Nicholas, was not in St. Louis.

Therefore, a move by me was imminent. It's possible I could've worked out the logistics to allow me to perform in *Hair* 2001, but there was another reason that kept me away.

As I've said, I always wanted to do *Hair*. And truth be told, I'd always wanted to perform the role of Berger—that free-spirited, make love not war, primordially driven wild man. And in the summer of 2000, I accomplished just that. But to do so, I had to confront a lot of characteristics and behaviors, emotions and issues I had experienced in the not so distant past. *Hair* 2000 was in no small part a huge therapy session for me. I learned a lot that summer—about myself, and about others. And I have Miller and the entire cast (and, of course, *Hair*) to thank.

But to reprise the role of Berger for another production would've tainted the seminal experience I had had. It would've been too painful, and I would not have been able to do the character, and ultimately the show, justice. The tools I had used to embody him were no longer available to me, and my performance would've been merely perfunctory. And to me, that is unacceptable.

However, I was able to come back and see *Hair* 2001 as an audience member. And Berger, Claude, the entire tribe and band were a treat to behold. They had taken it to yet another level. And that made me smile immensely.

I may never have the opportunity to work with Miller and New Line again, but I cherish the moment when I did. They do important work for the St. Louis community. They bring forth Honesty and Integrity with each production they stage. Support this company. Support the Arts. Without them, we are pedestrian. Without them, we are empty.

Peace and Love,
John Sparger
aka Sparger Berger
Hair 2000

I could scarcely contain my surprise when *Hair* really came together, and I do mean in a big way. Not only were our audiences totally digging our performances, but as a group, our Tribe was bonding in a way that no one expected. The myth that "doing *Hair* will change your life" was really true. I cried myself nearly to sickness and shrieked myself hoarse each night because the show and the pain of experiencing that life had become so real to me. I wasn't just playing Jeanie; I was her, and these were my dear friends who were being sent to fight a war, many never to return. And while I often can't verbalize the power this show has on those of us who are lucky enough to bring it to life, I choose to think of our Tribe as messengers. Messengers who had only one month to share our knowledge with as many people as we could.

—Beck Hunter, "Jeanie"

Scott Miller cast me in his 2000 New Line Theatre production of *Hair* as Claude despite the fact that I'm twice the age of the character and have short hair. The hair, as it turns out, was not such a big deal. Since Claude returns at the end of the play as a short-haired specter in an Army uniform, wearing a wig was very appropriate to play him. Now, I know nothing about wigs. Where would I go, then, to find a wig that would not only look good but would stand up to a punishing evening on stage?

Obviously, to a drag queen.

My friend, Michael, is well known in the St. Louis drag community as his alter ego, the ultra-glamorous Erica Fox. Since Erica had won the Miss Missouri Entertainer of the Year award on more than one occasion, I knew Michael/Erica would be my first choice as wig guru/gura.

"Sure, Ken, come on over!" Michael said when I called to ask his help. "I'm sure we can find *something* that'll work for you." When I arrived at his apartment, Michael had three or four wigs out on the kitchen table for us to consider. He gave me an appraising look and said, "I think this is the one for you." He picked up a center-parted, shoulder-length chestnut number and arranged it on my head. He stepped back and looked. "That's *it*!" he exclaimed, sweeping up the other wigs and putting them back in their boxes. "That's the wig for you."

"Really?" I asked, looking at my reflection in a hand mirror, unused to seeing my face framed by so much hair since I had been, well, Claude's age.

"Yes, really," he said, scooping it off my head. "Now, let me show you how to clean it." Clean it? There are instructions for how to clean it?

"First," he said, turning on the faucet in the kitchen sink, "fill the sink with warm water. Then add a capful of…"

"Shampoo?" I interrupted.

"No. Mr. Clean." He reached under the sink and poured the cleaning fluid into the sink.

"*Mr. Clean*!?!" I said, more loudly than I'd intended.

"Hon," he said, turning with a Bob Fosse hip-pop, the wig draped over his right hand, "this wig is made out of the same stuff as this floor," his left hand pointing at the linoleum. He turned back to the sink, demonstrating as he talked. "Place the wig in the water and gently swish it back and forth. Now run your fingers through it. As you lift it out, gently squeeze the water out. *Do not wring it out*! Now, to give it a really nice sheen, put fresh water in the sink and add a capful of…"

"Uh, conditioner?"

Michael gave me one of those how-could-someone-so-stupid-be-a-doctor looks. "No," he said slowly, "Murphy's Oil Soap."

"*Murphy's Oil Soap*!?!"

"Do you want my help or not?"

"Sorry."

He repeated the process with the furniture polish and concluded, "You dry it like this," taking the wig outside, holding it over his head, and slinging it forward and around with the force of a lesbian softball pitcher. He turned and looked at me sternly. "You *never* use a hair dryer. Why?"

"Uh, it would melt?"

He smiled. "Now you're getting it."

I followed Michael's regimen faithfully, subjecting the space-age polymer hairpiece to harsh chemicals before each weekend of our run, and, like the phoenix, it rose in glory each time.

While I'm sure the wig fooled no one into thinking I had seriously long hair, and while I'm sure no one thought I was really in my twenties, it all worked. When Claude returned to the stage in the final scene, dressed now in an army dress uniform, hair now in a buzz cut (my real hair, dyed to match the wig), I could hear people in the audience gasp, and as I sang the plaintive last reprise of "Manchester, England" in counterpoint to the protest song of the Tribe, I could hear them start to cry.

But that's New Line. While some people need chandeliers, roller skates, and helicopters, New Line just needs an authentic, aging hippie and a linoleum wig to create magic.

—Ken Haller, "Claude"

I put *Hair* into our season without really knowing much about it, aside from its more famous songs and its movie version, which I knew was very different than its stage incarnation. Luckily, early in the rehearsal process, I discovered online a discussion list about the show that included among its subscribers members of the original Broadway cast and Michael Butler, the show's original Broadway producer. Thank God for them. Learning the music was easy enough (though I'm glad I didn't have to memorize any of those list songs). But once we started blocking the show, I was lost. The script didn't make sense. There were virtually no stage directions. I found the archives of the discussion list and read every post. I started asking lots of questions. And slowly the show started making a little bit of sense. Their best advice was to Trust the Show. The rehearsal process became a kind of spiritual journey, a test of my trust. I did as they asked. I stopped worrying about the show. I stopped wondering how we would pull it off. I had trust. And I think it was that trust that kept the actors from freaking out completely. Despite the fact that they didn't think it could *ever* come together, they saw no worry in me. And sure enough, once we the put the show on its feet and once we got it in front of an audience, almost everything started making sense. We found all the emotion, all the spirituality, all the genius of this wild and weird show. But I owe Michael Butler, Nina, and others on that Internet list a great debt of gratitude. *Hair* changed my life.

—Scott Miller

A New Line Cabaret

◆

a world premiere
Featuring songs from past New Line shows, including
Songs for a New World, Company, Camelot, Attempting the Absurd, Into the Woods, Hair, Floyd Collins, Jacques Brel, Sweeney Todd, In the Blood, Pippin, and other shows
September 18-19, 2000
Sheldon Concert Hall, St. Louis

THE CAST
Karl Berberich, Chris Brenner, Colin DeVaughan, Cindy Duggan, Lisa Karpowicz, Robin Kelso, Robb Kennedy, Mo Monahan, Angie Shultz, John Rhine, Johanna Schloss, Leo Schloss, Deborah Sharn, Kimi Short, Keith Thompson

THE ARTISTIC STAFF
Directed by Scott Miller
Lighting Design by Amy Francis Schott

Cabaret

◆

Book and Lyrics by Fred Ebb
Music by John Kander
March 15-April 1, 2001
Art Loft Theatre, St. Louis

THE CAST

Cliff Bradshaw—Todd Schaefer
Ernst Ludwig—Christopher "Zany" Clark
Fraulein Schneider—Mo Monahan
Fraulein Kost—Deborah Sharn
Herr Schultz—Arthur Schwartz
Sally Bowles—Robin Kelso

The Kit Kat Klub

Emcee—Christopher Crivelli
Hansel/customs officer—Jim Hannah
Bobby—Bruce Ortiz
Victor—Terry L. Love
Rosie—Nicole Trueman
Lulu—Beck Hunter
Frenchie—Bradley Calise
Texas—Stacey Guenther

THE ARTISTIC STAFF
Director—Scott Miller
Assistant Director—Michael Leicht
Choreographer—JT Ricroft
Lighting Designer—Mark Schilling
Set Designer—Todd Schaefer
Costume Designer—Betsy Krausnick
Stage Manager—Amy Francis Schott
Master Electrician—Tim Lord
Box Office Manager—Steve Dohrmann
Graphic Designer—Kris Wright
Photography—Robert Stevens

THE BAND
Piano—Brad Hofeditz
Trumpet—Paul Hecht
Trombone—Jim Shiels
Bass—Terry Kippenberger
Percussion—Adam Kopff

THE REVIEWS
"A small spotlight falls on a door, slightly ajar. A hand reaches out, showing off black-polished nails. The index finger beckons seductively. Then the middle finger signals. With that opening moment, director Scott Miller condenses his entire approach of *Cabaret*—tempting, vulgar, shrewdly theatrical and admirably economical. It's one of the most powerful productions that Miller's company, New Line Theatre, has ever staged…[The band's] raw sound suits the mood that Miller and choreographer JT Ricroft evoke in steamy Klub numbers like 'Money' and 'Two Ladies,' visually exciting and metaphorically explicit. We're in a very sick world…Christopher Crivelli's venomous performance as the Kit Kat emcee sets the standard for this show—leering, cold, totally in control.

Robin Kelso plays the English star of the club, Sally Bowles, with a lot of flair both in her 'onstage' scenes (more pose than talent) and her 'offstage' scenes (more pose than heart). Yet her winning, tiny smile, coupled with occasional bursts of warmth, complicates the character. You can't dismiss her, and you can't trust her. It's a provocative combination…But the cold heart of the play lies in the Kit Kat Klub ensemble, whose entertainments reveal a morally bereft world-view that still can frighten us. And should."—Judith Newmark, *St. Louis Post-Dispatch*

"I'm sitting in the front row of the most remarkable production to hit St. Louis this season…We're close enough that this once familiar musical is transformed into something quite unlike any production of it you may have seen. It's *Cabaret* . . And it's one of the best things I've seen the New Line Theatre do…Director Scott Miller has made his New Line Theatre a St. Louis institution, and I'm happy to see that it has so vibrantly survived the loss of the St. Marcus. It is very much at home in the Art Loft Theatre on Washington. Besides his deep understanding of musical theatre, Miller's chief gift, I think, is for the gathering of outstanding talent."—Steve Callahan, KDHX-FM

"A must-see for anyone who is interested in theatre in St. Louis."—Gerry Kowarsky, *St. Louis Post-Dispatch*

"*Cabaret*, at the New Line Theatre, is a flawed but noteworthy production of the groundbreaking musical, which is as fresh and provocative as it was when it was created in 1966. The production is at its strongest in the musical numbers, all staged deftly on the tiny club-like stage by director Scott Miller and choreographer JT Ricroft. Vocally, the cast is first-rate [and] the band excellent (the accordion is a nice touch)…In the opening number, 'Wilkommen,' the over-rouged, zombielike Kit Kat girls and boys, and their Emcee (Christopher Crivelli) perform enough pelvic thrusts and simulated oral sex for several productions. We're supposed to be shocked,

shocked, but the gestures are so mechanical and contrived that they become boring and meaningless. Perhaps that's what director Miller intended: Sex has become common currency, as devalued as the German mark."—Brian Hohlfeld, *The Riverfront Times*

DIRECTOR'S NOTES

Why is New Line Theatre, a company known for presenting world premieres and St. Louis premieres of new works, producing a thirty-five-year-old musical? That's simple. Because it still matters. Because there are some lessons in life so important we must revisit them from time to time.

So what does *Cabaret* have to teach us in 2001? That it's not okay to ignore what's going on around us; that we cannot allow our world to be less than it should be; that we should never keep quiet; that it's important to participate; that we have a responsibility to each other and to our community; that any discrimination, any indignity, any prejudice, no matter how slight, must be brought out into the light of day and condemned.

What would have happened in Germany in the early 1930s if more people had voted? What would have happened if people like Sally Bowles had paid attention to what was happening in the Reichstag? What would have happened if people like Fraulein Schneider had stood up and said loudly and decisively that they will *not* accept intimidation, that they will *not* be bullied, that they will *not* go along in the name of self-preservation? What would have happened if the people of Germany had listened more closely to the Nazis and then stood up and denounced Adolf Hitler for the madman he was?

Would things have been different? I really don't know.

But there was some moment, some point of no return, when the Germans could have gone down a different road and saved the world from the horrors that should not have been inevitable.

Cabaret is about that moment, a time when it wasn't yet too late, when Germany wasn't yet locked into the path that would lead to the murder of millions of Jews. But the people of Germany couldn't see what we see. They didn't know how their choices, their fears, their apathy would lead to bigger things. People like Fraulein Schneider and Fraulein Kost were busy just trying to survive. People like Sally Bowles were busy having too good a time.

The extermination of the Jews started small, in tiny, daily indignities; in little, nearly unnoticeable acts of prejudice; in seemingly innocent jokes; in the words people chose. Could the same thing happen today? Of course it could. Right-wing political leaders in America today say pretty much the same things the Nazis said about gays, women, family, religion, culture, education, and patriotism. It may not seem dangerous right now, but it didn't seem dangerous in Germany in 1930 either.

We have an obligation to learn from what happened in Germany. We have an obligation to make different choices. If we don't do it today, it may be too late tomorrow.

REMEMBERING CABARET

What an incredible experience this was for me. I had the distinct pleasure of being involved with one of the most talented group of people I have ever worked with—their creativity; their openness and responsiveness made *Cabaret* an event in my life that I will never forget.

I was given the role of the Emcee. It was a role of a lifetime. Now, I am keeping this all in its proper perspective. This is a professional company that uses this small space in downtown St. Louis. This is certainly not the big league. However, given the quality of the production, it very well could have been.

I auditioned for Scott Miller, and all the while I was thinking about Joel Grey in the movie. Mind you, I had not seen the stage revival. I was cast, and soon after, we had our first rehearsal. At that time, JT Ricroft, our choreographer *extraordinaire*, came to me and said, "In this number (Two Ladies), we would like for you to drop your pants and show your bare butt to the audience. Oh, and you need to grab each other's crotches in one part of the song as well." Okay, this was not the Joel Grey Emcee. I think I just entered a new dimension, and I am in for a wild ride. And I was right.

Scott's vision of this production took all of us into the dark, deep, and seedy side of Berlin in the early 1930s. He opened doors for all of us, digging into our fantasies and stretching us all in body and mind. This was an amazing group of actors that just clicked. The result was an outstanding production which left a lasting impression on us all, one that we will rarely be able to duplicate in our lifetimes.

Scott knows how I feel about him as an artist and as a person. He gave me the ability to create and to stretch myself as an actor beyond what I thought I was able to accomplish. The fulfillment is one that I will keep with me forever. For the past twenty years I had dreamed of playing this role, and Scott allowed this small dream to be realized.

I personally have to thank Scott for his artistry in making this a special experience for me, and I know I can speak for the rest of the cast as well. New Line is a great venue for pushing the limits of theater. And with Scott at the helm, I know the St. Louis audience will experience the very edges of theater for years to come. I can't wait to be part of the next New Line experience.

—Christopher Crivelli, "Emcee"

Betsy, the costumer, was at rehearsal to take measurements for the costumes. She entered the room just as we were beginning to run the opening number, "Wilkommen." I hadn't seen Betsy in quite some time, so I went over to say hello and tell her how happy I was to see her. I knew she was there for costuming, but she had no idea why I was there. Actually, she thought I was *in* the show. As the number progressed, I noticed a look of horror on her face. At first I thought she wasn't feeling well, until she leaned over and asked me a question, somewhat in confidence: "What sick mind created that number?" After showing a guilty grin and feeling satisfied that I had received my first confirmation that the number was going to work, I looked at her and simply smiled. No words were necessary. Ahhh, my work is complete.

—John Ricroft, choreographer

Life is a *grope-fest*, ol' chum. That's right. Grope-fest. I've never before been rubbed on, rubbed myself on, and groped so many so often. When J.T. began to teach us the choreography for the opening number, "Wilkommen," everyone was a little hesitant at first. After a shy crotch grab here, and a nipple tweak there, the awkwardness dissolved. By the end of the run, grinding on someone was second nature. I've also never before or since had the pleasure to work with such a talented group of people, across the board. Every single actor with whom I shared the stage had something unique and amazing to bring to the production. The direction, choreography, the band—it was all pretty amazing. From on stage to behind the scenes. And speaking of backstage, one of my favorite backstage antics had to have been the "boy ballet"—Terry would partner Bruce during "Why Should I Wake Up?" It was really quite lovely.

—Stacey Guenther, "Texas"

I remember staging the opening number, "Wilkommen." I knew I wanted to make a statement during the first few minutes. How can I capture the audience's attention and accurately portray the decadence of that time and place that's so important to the story? Simulated Sex on Stage! Yeah, that's the ticket! So, I asked the chorus to break up into groups of twos and threes, so that we had three clusters around the stage. I then asked each group to come up with three "positions" that would present a graphic picture and I gave them fifteen minutes. During this time, I began to feel concerned about two cast members (Bruce and Steve) who were rather young, and were off on their own. They were talking to each other quietly and looking somewhat confused. I began thinking, would they be able to create something that fit the rest of the group? I went to each group and asked them to strike each position on count. Group 1, GO! Great job! Group 2, GO! Again, perfect. Okay, now it's Bruce and Steve's turn to show their stuff (no pun intended). I was fully prepared to witness something that would need some help and be adjusted. I just *knew* that they weren't going to be able to come up with something. Group 3, GO! Much to my surprise, they did just fine. All I remember is during the two other groups' turns at displaying their "acts," there was tons of laughter and joking. Once Bruce and Steve began, I heard complete silence. The room was speechless and shocked. Mouths were open in amazement. It was perfectly clear that Bruce and Steve knew *exactly* what they were doing…

—John Ricroft, choreographer

Anyone Can Whistle

◆

Music and Lyrics by Stephen Sondheim
Book by Arthur Laurents
June 14-30, 2001
Art Loft Theatre, St. Louis

THE CAST
Mayoress Cora Hoover Hooper—Lisa Karpowicz
J. Bowden Hapgood—Troy Schnider
Nurse Fay Apple—Chelsea Phillips
Comptroller Schub—Michael Brightman
Treasurer Cooley—Paul Coffman
Chief of Police Magruder—Christopher Clark
Cora's Bodyguard—Greg Coleman
Mrs. Schroeder—Cindy Duggan
Baby Joan Schroeder—Jeannie Skala
Dr. Detmold—Terry Meddows
Kiné Brown, Justin Heinrich, Alison Helmer, Tamara Kelly,
Uchenna Ogu

THE ARTISTIC STAFF
Director—Scott Miller
Choreographer—JT Ricroft
Lighting Designer—Tim Lord

Set Supervisor—Christopher Clark
Miracle Rock & Puppet Design—Todd Schaefer
Costume Designer—Russell J. Bettlach
Hair Design—Ren Binder
Box Office Manager—Steve Dohrmann
Graphic Designer—Kris Wright
Photography—Robert Stevens

THE BAND
Piano—Neal Richardson
Trumpet—Carl Nelson
Percussion—Adam Kopff

THE REVIEWS

"Instead of bringing serious matters to the foreground, as he often does, director Scott Miller went all out for entertainment and let the issues emerge from a framework of farce. The resulting show offered much to enjoy on the surface without obscuring the depth."—Gerry Kowarksy, *The Sondheim Review*

"The best reason to see *Anyone Can Whistle*, the appealing mess of a show that New Line Theatre is staging at the ArtLoft, is simple. You're not likely to get another chance…Still, anything by Stephen Sondheim has an element of fascination, thanks to his enormous influence on modern musical theatre. New Line's artistic director Scott Miller, who has staged a number of Sondheim shows, directs this one with verve and intelligence…Miller and choreographer JT Ricroft make the most of the ArtLoft's flexible space."—Judith Newmark, *St. Louis Post-Dispatch*

"In some respects, things have gone downhill in the last 37 years for the show…On the other hand, it's a chance to see what the young Sondheim was capable of doing. There are a few excellent songs and some imaginative staging by Miller, and some of the comedy, led by Michael Brightman as Comptroller Schub, is delightful."—Joe Pollack, KWMU-FM

"[Director Scott] Miller and choreographer JT Ricroft stage the musical numbers with brio—nicely adapting to the ArtLoft's shallow stage and making intriguing use of aisle space."—Cliff Froehlich, *The Riverfront Times*

DIRECTOR'S NOTES

When *Anyone Can Whistle* opened in 1964, it was so bizarre in its style, so savage in its satire, so outrageous in its social commentary that it ran only nine performances. It attacked the commercialization of religion, which still persists today, the gender and racial stereotypes that go unchallenged still today, and the blatant corruption and profiteering of politicians, which is worse today than ever. In short, it attacked the way its audiences lived their lives. No wonder it closed in a week. Musicals didn't do that in 1964.

But the truth is those lives deserved attack, and our lives today deserve the attack even more. How is it that we condone the fact that religious titans Pat Robertson, Jerry Falwell, and Jesse Jackson are millionaires and live in mansions? What would Jesus or Gandhi have said about that? How do we condone the outrageous black stereotypes that still pervade television and movies? What would Booker T. Washington and Martin Luther King, Jr. have said about the over-sexed, drugged-out, brainless comedies full of negative stereotypes that African-American writers and actors are churning out week after week? How do we condone the fact that the president of the United States, a card—carrying member of the oil industry, wants to drill in the Arctic National Preserve, so he and his friends can make money? Is he all that different from Mayoress Cora Hoover Hooper?

Stephen Sondheim and Arthur Laurents address these outrages by shining the harsh light of satire on them, exaggerating them and making the insanity and insidiousness of these practices crystal clear to us all. Cora's fake miracle gets us thinking about Dubya and his oil buddies. The black woman Martha's stereotypical "black" dialect and her musical references to *Porgy and Bess* make us recognize how readily we accept black stereotypes in everyday life—still today—without even realizing it. June and John's gender bending shows us how silly and outdated gender roles are in our society and how far we *haven't* come since the 1950s. Fay's sex-only-by-disguise points up the hypocrisy and hang-ups Americans have over sexuality. The Cookies themselves show us how quickly we label any deviation from the norm as a sickness or disability of some sort.

Yes, this show may offend you a little, but if that's the only way to get us all thinking about what's wrong with our culture, then so be it. Our world is a mess, and if we can laugh tonight at how ridiculous we all are, maybe tomorrow morning we can start making changes. *Anyone Can Whistle* creates a strange relationship between the observers and the observed. You sit watching the kooky inhabitants of Cora's town, but *Anyone Can Whistle* is also watching us, noticing every prejudice, every injustice, every ridiculous and selfish move we make in our everyday lives. And at the end of Act I, we're forced to ask the literal question: who's watching whom?

So why is the show called *Anyone Can Whistle*? I think it's because this show is about the choices we make every day, about whether we do what we're told or just go on our merry way, living life in our own quirky fashion. Whistling is a symbol of freedom, abandon, fun, and stubborn nonconformity. Most people don't chase after those things. But anyone can.

REMEMBERING ANYONE CAN WHISTLE

Like several other shows we've done, *Anyone Can Whistle* scared the shit out of me until the second week of the run, when our audiences *finally* started laughing their heads off. But I've become a fear junkie—if it doesn't terrify me, if it doesn't challenge me, if it doesn't ask things of me that have never been asked before, it isn't really fun. I didn't know if my ideas for *Whistle* would work and if audiences and reviewers would understand and embrace my take on this very bizarre absurdist musical. That first week of performances, I honestly thought I might be the only person on earth who thought this show was really funny. I asked for ridiculous, over-sized, manic performances, and the actors trusted me and gave me those performances. The audiences barely laughed that first week, but the actors still trusted me. We got mixed reviews, but they still trusted me. They trusted me and I trusted the material and that's the only way to do theatre.

Anyone Can Whistle represents everything New Line Theatre is about—rule-busting, aggressively screwing with audience expectations, refusing to do what's been done before, tackling difficult material that scares everybody else, demanding that audiences *think* and *participate* in the experience of live theatre. And the truth is that even if all our audiences had greeted our show with only mild chuckles—or even outright hostility—I still would have been proud of us. This show was good and the hell with anybody who says differently. They haven't taken the time to really see all the treasure that is there, and it's their loss. And not only was the show good, it's also important. As I said in my program notes, maybe if we can see how ridiculous our world is, we'll be motivated to make it better. Theatre is not just about entertainment; it's about coming together as a community to discuss the things that need discussing. If we can't make a difference, if we can't make people think, if we can't change the world, why are we wasting our time?

—Scott Miller, director

When Scott cast me in *Anyone Can Whistle*, I must admit to having been both excited and disappointed. I was disappointed because I had hoped to snag the leading role of Hapgood. It was a reality shock to me that I had to face the fact that at 36, I was probably too old now to play the "ingénue" roles, such as Hapgood; but felt surely I was not ready to begin playing the older, character roles; the roles I refer to as "The Mr. Mooney" roles. The shock of being cast came because I really didn't think I would get cast in *any* role! Although I gave what I thought was a good audition, I had some conflicts with the rehearsal schedule, and felt that it would prevent my being cast in such a large role as Comptroller Schub. But cast I was. And what a phenomenal role it turned out to be for me. I didn't know that I had it in me to play this guy the way I played him. I had a blast! Looking back, I would have never even considered playing Hapgood if I had known what fun it could be to be Mr. Mooney! I learned a great deal from doing this show, but what I learned the most is that the largest role is *not* always the best role!

—Michael Brightman, "Comptroller Schub"

I really never thought I would write a piece like this about a professional theatre director. Contrary to popular belief, working with professionals doesn't always mean you get a professional environment. It was for this reason I took a very long hiatus from musical theater after doing a full summer run of *Oklahoma!* in Florida. I was burned out, empty, and felt that the creative atmosphere of theatre was gone. The creative process, which I had embraced during my undergraduate studies, was displaced by budgets, production schedules, and directors who espoused logic but failed to convey art in their productions, much less protect their actors. I was also tired of this kind of direction from almost every single director I worked with: "If I'm not telling you that you're doing anything wrong, you're doing okay." Who really wants to be just okay?

This brings me to Scott Miller. A mutual friend encouraged me to give New Line Theatre a go. I walked into the audition and proceeded to sing a song that didn't sound too hard on the ears, and performed my greatest acting coup ever by convincing Scott and JT that I was a comedic actor. The fools! What separated the New Line experience for me was it felt like a return to my undergraduate years. It felt safe to experiment, play, and try different things night after night. If we went too far, Scott was there to catch us. If we weren't going far enough, he would encourage us to go further.

I will carry two memories away from the show. The first memory is when the audience seemed to have finally gotten the show and they were responding with smiles and loud guffaws. It proved that the critics were wrong and somehow a lot of people in the past missed the genius of Sondheim and Laurents in this piece. What is the second memory? Scott Miller trying to find ways to get me in trouble by wondering out loud which female cast member was in my sights for that night.

—Paul Coffman, "Treasurer Cooley"

"What the hell have I gotten myself into!" Those were the first words I mumbled to myself as I was leaving the first read-through of *Anyone Can Whistle*. I could not believe that a director could read that script and still want to so passionately perform it in front of a viewing audience.

When I got home I read the script again, discussed it with my family and my friends, still not getting an answer that satisfied me as to why I should continue with this production. Finally, I got the courage to e-mail Scott about it. (Some courage, e-mail.) I had no idea what his reaction would be; after all, this was my first production with New Line. But this play sparked such a fire in me, I had to say something.

The next day I checked my e-mail. There it was, the response. I was so nervous to open it because I thought, he's going to think of me as a trouble maker and kick me out of the show. So, I opened it.

The message started off with some background knowledge about the play, which I already knew from reading the information I had received at the read-through. As I continued to read on, I got to the last couple of lines which read, "Theatre is not always meant to be comfortable. Sometimes it is uncomfortable and that is why we do it, to challenge ourselves as well as the audience." After reading that, I had no doubt in my mind that I would do the show.

The funny thing about this situation was that I knew that about theatre. I have even done a "heated" play before about the struggle in Ireland during the World Wars. That did not affect me like *Whistle*. Then I thought about it. *Whistle* was directly making fun of all the racial stereotypes that were placed on us back then in the 60s that we still have yet to overcome today.

Once I got past that, I really began to play with the script as far as character choices were concerned. I will admit that I was still nervous about the show. Every rehearsal Scott would say, "I reeeeally need you guys to go to the extreme. Nothing can be too much for this show. Don't focus on the offensiveness; I know it is offensive; just play past it and accept it." When Scott said that, I began to trust him because he trusted Sondheim, and that was all I needed to worry about.

When that show opened, we did not at all know how that audience would respond to the show. Scott was even a little nervous, but once we opened, I think all of a sudden it just clicked for everyone. It was so AWESOME!!! From the characters, to the pace, to the lines, to the music! Don't get me wrong; I felt good about it in rehearsal, but the audience really made the difference, especially in this show. I am glad that I stuck with it.

—Tamara L. Kelly

*H*air

Book and Lyrics by Gerome Ragni and James Rado
Music by Galt MacDermot
July 26-September 1, 2001
ArtLoft Theatre, St. Louis

THE OSAGE TRIBE
(and their chosen tribe names)
Kiné Brown (Venus Love Child), Bradley Calise (Moses), Joy Ducree (Songbird), Wayne Easter (Zion), Mike Heeter (Capt. Britannica), Justin Heinrich (Knight of Cups), Mike Howard (Nougat), Beck Hunter (Li'l Boll Weevil), Tamara Kelly (Dances with Freedom), Terry L. Love (Monsoon), Mo Monahan (Mother Nature), Uchenna Ogu (Marrakesh), John Rhine (Priest), Nicole Trueman (Sun)

THE ARTISTIC STAFF
Director/Music Director—Scott Miller (Kerouac)
Lighting Designer—Paul Summers (Rabbi)
Costume Designers—Justin Heinrich & Bradley Calise
Set Designer & Scene Painter—The Osage Tribe
Stage Manager—Chris "Zany" Clark (Lightning Bug)
Box Office Manager—Steve Dohrmann (Soaring Eagle)

THE BAND

Piano/Conductor—Scott Miller
Lead Guitar—Dale Hampton
Rhythm Guitar—M. Joshua Ryan
Bass—Dave Hall
Trumpet—Carl Nelson
Percussion—Adam Kopff

THE REVIEWS

"New Line's production…forged an intense connection with its audience…The finale, 'Let the Sun Shine In,' was almost unbearably emotional. and brought the audience onto the stage to tearfully hug and dance with the cast."—Allison Xantha Miller, *American Theatre Magazine*

"When a director revives a play less than a year after he first staged it, he better have good reason—reasons like style, audience appeal and abundant energy. New Line artistic director Scott Miller has all the reason he needs for this summer's revival of last summer's hit, *Hair*…[It] is, above all, an ensemble piece. It emerged from a time when it seemed possible that group efforts to change society could succeed. This play, and New Line's production of it, succeed on exactly those same terms."—Judith Newmark, *St. Louis Post-Dispatch*

"Director Scott Miller's Osage Tribe is an ensemble cast of frenzied and frolicking psychedelic-perfection…The Osage shout, scream, wail, sing, point, dance, laugh, plead, and rage to the audience that is intimately wrapped around the stage like some morphed tribal council in trance. It is wondrous…But it is the Osage ensemble that is the real star. Their unbridled energy and communal vocals framed within Miller's imaginative choreography provide a manic tale that when finished finds you somewhere in between tears and euphoric joy."—Colin Murphy, *The Vital Voice*

"Don't let the language and the nude scene fool you—there's a lot of innocence and idealism on the stage, and those are two things we need—any time—whether with *Hair* or without."—Joe Pollack, KWMU-FM

"New Line Theatre shows off its crowning glory in an open-ended run of *Hair*."—Byron Kerman, *The Riverfront Times*

"Artistically, [*Hair* in June 2000] was one of the best productions New Line ever staged, and everybody seemed to know it."—Judith Newmark, *St. Louis Post-Dispatch*

DIRECTOR'S NOTES

It is 1968 and the youth of America are lost.

Their parents, still celebrating the prosperity that followed World War II, have raised social drinking to an art form; they are bathing in the excesses of capitalistic materialism, and they are showering their children with everything anyone could want—except the nourishment of the soul.

These young people have all the physical trappings of happiness but don't know who they are, where they belong, what is expected of them. More of them are going to college than ever before, where they learn to think independently, to question the status quo, and to reject their parents' long-held, arbitrary definitions of morality, success, and happiness. These young people see racism run rampant in America, with lynchings still common in the South. They see American youths shipped off to southeast Asia to fight a war which has nothing to do with America and which appears to be unjust, immoral, racist, and impossible to win. They see disregard for the environment in the unchecked progress of American industry. And they see a culture that now worships at the feet of a new God—consumerism.

What do these kids want? They want to erase all the rules and start over, creating a new society that makes sense; one built on the idea of celebrating all the wonderful, magical, indefinable things that make us human; the things that unite us; the things that join us to the rest of the natural world. They ask why we have such restrictive rules of sexuality. Is it because some culture from long ago wanted to control inheritance? Or was it about the perpetuating of a particular ethnic group? Why do we have such restrictive rules about drugs? Is it because once we taste the liberation of mind-expanding substances, we'll be harder to control? Why do the adults who drink like fishes at cocktail parties so self-righteously condemn marijuana? Why do they so strongly condemn all drugs, when so many other cultures highly value the ritual use of hallucinogenic drugs to achieve a higher level of consciousness and to find God? Why do so many people call themselves people of faith but act in such immoral ways?

Our tribe has not come to insult you or the values you hold dear. Our intention is not to shock or upset—though we may do that too. We have come to celebrate our humanness, the joy of living, our connection to each other and to the world around us, our God-given sexuality, and the wonders and mysteries of the human mind and body We have come to ask you to join us in rejecting violence, hatred, fear, and judgment wherever we find it; to question the way things have always been; to look at the world with a fresh eye, and to resolve to change the things that need changing.

Especially here and now, in the year 2001, consider whether we need more guns in the world, whether we value our children enough, whether we value our freedom enough, whether we value our planet enough, and whether people should be discriminated against because of the way they look or who they fall in love with.

It is a new age. Everything is ready. It's time to change the world.

REMEMBERING HAIR

After my first show with New Line, *Anyone Can Whistle*, I took a psychedelic trip up the Methedrine River to *Hair*. I could not believe that I got to do this show. I wanted to do this show ever since I was in college. I said that if anyone ever did it, I would be in it. Well, a year before doing *Whistle*, I was skimming through the *Riverfront Times* and found that New Line Theatre was having auditions for *Hair*. I thought the mother ship had landed and it was calling me home. But I was not prepared for the audition at all, so I didn't go.

Then, as *Whistle* was closing, some of the cast members went into rehearsal for *Hair* again. I found out that they were making some changes to the show, and that is when I seized the day. I said to Scott, "If you need one more person, I will be glad to be in it." I could tell that Scott was in serious debate about letting one more person into the show because the other four new people had already had rehearsals with the previous year's cast. Let me tell you, I was on pins and needles waiting for him to say something about it. Nothing. Didn't hear anything for a while. Then finally I was asked to join the *Hair* cast, and as professionally as I could, I said, "Yes." (On the inside I was pissing my pants.)

Later during the run of *Whistle*, some of the last year's *Hair* cast come to see us. I was so nervous because they didn't know anything about me; I didn't know anything about them; I just didn't know what to expect. When I met them, they were so friendly and welcoming of me, I knew everything was going to be all right. I will have to keep it real—I was a little overwhelmed by the words in the songs, but everyone made sure to let me know that if I needed any help, just ask.

Early in the rehearsal process, I felt an immediate closeness among the cast even though we were still getting to know each other. We became such a family even down to the little disagreements we would have. It was funny how one show could bring strangers so close together to form bonds that last a lifetime.

There is a reason that I found New Line and Scott at this point in my life. And I think that the reason is very simple. It was time for me to grow up and realize who I am and who I am becoming. I know that might sound strange, but working with this company, in these two shows, through the allowance of Scott, I will never be the same again. Thank you, Scott!

—Tamara L. Kelly
Osage Tribe name "Dances with Freedom"

As with every family in the 1960s, our lives were changed by the Vietnam War. What was once a typical family of kids going to high school, school plays, and sports had turned into a life of impending doom. My two older brothers were drafted into the army. Our home was filled with quiet fear of the dreaded phone call that they were "going over." No one really talked about it until the letters from their friends who were there were sent. Here I was, a little girl, listening to stories of shrapnel imbedded in the arms, legs, and faces of the boys I've known all my life. I tried to escape from the nightmare of what was happening around me. But how could I? Dan Rather, war correspondent, was showing me images every night on the news of bloody bodies, stories of torture, POWs, and the horrors of "the real world." I felt utterly confused, helpless, and totally freaked out that my brothers may be included in the body count of the dead. Children should not believe that war is a part of life. I thought every generation *had* to have a war. After all, my grandfather was in WWI and my dad in WWII. Doing *Hair* helped me break out and shout to the world to stop the violence, stop the prejudice. *Hair* gave me hope of peace and the realization that I can make a difference. I finally can speak out and express the emotions that I kept inside of me, so tormented, at the age of twelve. I am a new person because of *Hair*. The Osage Tribe has a motto to "Keep It Real." If we speak out about the injustices of the world, someone will listen. The audience listened, and I felt empowered and it has overflowed into my life and I will never be the same. My brothers, Pat and Dan, never were shipped over. By some miracle of fate, they were saved and I am thankful.

—Mo Monahan
Osage Tribe name "Mother Nature"

It's impossible to describe the experience of performing *Hair* to someone who hasn't done it. I was highly skeptical of the many people who told me their lives were changed by working on this show—until I worked on it, that is. From the choosing of the tribe name to the overwhelming, almost unbearable rush of emotion in the show's finale, it is an experience unlike any other. Not only does it bond each member of the tribe to every other member (and this includes actors, director, designers, musicians, box office people), but it bonds each tribe to all the other tribes around the world, past and present. It centers people, changes them, guides them toward balance in their lives, guides them back to paths in their lives they've forgotten or abandoned, guides them toward a deeper spirituality, one that may or may not have to do with Christianity. Even the most cynical among us was transformed by *Hair*. It holds a mystical, primal power that is impossible to explain. Just as it is utterly unique in so many concrete ways, it is just as unique in all the unexplainable ways. And because we closed this second production of the show just nine days before the infamous terrorist attacks on the World Trade Center towers and the Pentagon, it shaped profoundly how we reacted to that event as well. We talked a lot about that among the tribe. We felt like we all had an additional shield against the attack on America, a shield the rest of the country didn't know about—as Hallmarky as it may sound, we had the power and the peace of *Hair* to get us through that. Michael Butler, the original Broadway producer of *Hair*, had told me when he flew in to see our show that he believed another 60s era was coming and that the *Hair* tribes would lead the way. Certainly, when the U.S. declared war on September 11, we all saw parallels to Vietnam and we wondered how he knew.

—Scott Miller, director
Osage Tribe name "Kerouac"

And what of LSD? Is it just a drug, or the reason a group of children grew flowers in their hair, had stars in the eyes, and thought they could change the world? If they knew then what they know now, would they still have tasted those sweetened drops, or would they have laid down in the transcendental river of reality and let it wash them away—daisies and all?

What a crazy time that was. Whoo! But did we dig it then and do we dig it now? We do. And if I meet up with Scott Miller in St. Louis, I definitely will say thanks for letting me put the flowers back into my hair and keep the starlight in my eyes for two summers now. And I'll probably let him know that I dig all of the time he spent researching those cats and their message, so we could stay true to their power. Boom boom, beep beep.

And so maybe they really will change the world after all—just not as quickly as they had hoped because they didn't foresee the need to hand the daisy-powered baton to the next generation. And so maybe the journey of these past two summers of love are not at the beginning or the end, but just another piece of that movement. And maybe when Scott and the rest of the tribe look in the mirror, they'll notice the stars and they'll keep on passing out flowers and won't put them down for a long time to come.

Our destination is the same—our journey is where it's at and we all know where it's at. Let the sun shine in. Peace and love.

—Uchenna Ogu
Osage Tribe name "Marrakesh"

Yes, *Hair* changed my life.

Now that I have that out of the way, I figure I'm faced with two choices. I could either: A) spend the rest of this essay attempting to articulate just how *Hair* has made me a more caring yet carefree person with an amazing renewed spirit, *blah, blah, blah*; or, B) I could describe a single incident that kinda sums up all of those things in a nice neat package. While A is a tempting, I think I'll keep it simple for this assignment and go with the answer I always chose when I couldn't come up with something better on high school history tests: B.

"Can I have your headband?"

It seemed like an innocent enough request from the sweet, smiling, grandma-type standing in front of me after our final *Hair* performance, September 1, 2001. Following nearly every show, the scene was similar—people pouring out of their seats to fill the stage floor, dancing with the cast, hugging, crying and telling their own stories of the Johnson/Nixon Era. But this woman's agenda was different. She tapped me on the shoulder, turned me around to face her and grabbed my hands. She just stared at me with wet eyes for what was beginning to be an uncomfortable amount of time. She said nothing. She followed it up with a surprisingly strong hug and finally the question—"Can I have your headband?"

Playing Claude in our production, I found that people had strange reactions to me after the show. Having just seen Claude murdered in the jungles of Vietnam, only to appear once more as a ghostly vision, some people were hesitant to talk to me. Some wouldn't even make eye contact. But there were others still who only wanted to tell me about their personal Vietnam experiences—the political atmosphere in the late 60s and early 70s, the horrible memories of the draft, and the young people they lost to Vietnam.

But this woman wanted my headband—a simple, red, western patterned handkerchief that I had folded to tie around my head. It was used to reflect the fashion of the period, but mostly I tied it on to hold my wig tightly in place. "I would love for you to have it." I said, and walked with her on my arm to the backstage area. Along the way, she told me how much she enjoyed the show, how it made her feel and about the 19-year-old son that she lost to Vietnam. As she took the headband from me, she again grabbed my hands and said, "My son used to wear a headband just like this, and I wanted to keep it to help me remember."

My mind went numb. Nothing I could've said would have made a difference anyway. It just sent a breaker of emotion that started at the base of my neck, up and over my head like a hood. I had no use for the headband any longer. The show was over and it was time to move on. I just thanked the woman for coming to the show, hugged her and zombied upstairs to the dressing rooms.

As I stripped out of my character's final soldier's dress uniform and began putting on my "real world" clothes of jeans, tennis shoes and a t-shirt, it smacked me hard. The idea that *Hair* wasn't just some relic of 60s flower power. Its effects have reached way beyond that. This show that seems so dated on the exterior, but it's still having a profound effect on every member of its audience and anyone involved in its production. This woman's simple request broke through my opaque walls and the sun came piercing through. Taking stock, re-prioritizing, and connecting with people in ways I had long forgotten—it's all in my future now. I'm following the river in my heart. Down to the gutter. Up to the glitter. Into the city where the truth lies. Thank you *Hair*. Thank you God. And thank you to the nameless woman who showed me the way.

—Mike Heeter, "Claude"
Osage Tribe name Capt. Britannica

Move On
Notes from the Artistic Director

♦

When I founded New Line Theatre in 1991, it was Stephen Sondheim's words, fittingly enough, that kept whispering in my ears:
> *Anything you do,*
> *Let it come from you.*
> *Then it will be new.*
> *Give us more to see...*

And I have tried to live up to those words by challenging myself and the artists of New Line every chance I get, to ask more of us than we think we can give, to scare the hell out of us on a regular basis. After directing *Sweeney Todd* in 1996, I realized it's not really all that much fun anymore unless I'm terrified. That terror not only keeps me working my hardest, but it also forces me to be creative, to find unexpected solutions to unexpected problems; and New Line's continued success, even with the most difficult shows, has shown me how to have faith in myself and those around me, to believe that even though I can't see the answers right now, the answers are there and we will find them.

The theatre is my church and I am definitely a person of faith. I don't say that casually. When I hear people describe deeply religious experiences, when they talk about the overwhelming emotion, the power, the transcendence of knowing God, that's what I feel in the theatre. There is a connection, not only between the actors, but to the audience and in a very real sense, to all of humankind. When we produced *Floyd Collins*, we connected to every family who has ever lost a loved one; we felt them, we knew them, we could touch them. And we also connected to the real Floyd Collins and his friends and family, his neighbors and those who only barely knew him. We inhabited those people and we saw the world through their eyes. We felt their pain, their hope, their faith. And when Floyd spoke to God at the end of the show, when he made his way to heaven, we all touched God as well.

We touch God every time we take the stage, even when we're doing shows that "religious" people won't like. It is always a religious experience in the realest possible sense. Stephen Sondheim once said that to live in music is a gift from God. And the theatre is my church.

Yes, we sometimes deal in sexuality and in obscenity. We deal in violence and darkness. We deal in *all* that is real and human. We revel in the fascinating complexity that is the human creation. Sexuality is not bad; it's human expression and connection and love and life. Obscene words are not bad; they're just words, no better or worse than the intentions behind them. And the only way to understand ourselves and the world around us is to look at it, *all* of it, not just the parts that don't scare us. If we refuse to look at the scary parts, we'll never learn to overcome them. In this country of ours, with too many guns, too much anger, and too much violence, I believe high schools should all be required to produce Sondheim's *Assassins* every four years. We'll never stop our children from killing each other by ignoring their screams of agony. We'll only stop the violence if we can understand it. As Sondheim has said many times, art makes order out of the chaos of our lives. The better we can understand our lives, the better we can live them. And nothing can illuminate the mysteries of the human mind and heart better than musical theatre.

Though we haven't yet produced Sondheim's masterpiece *Sunday in the Park with George* (don't worry, we'll get to it), we have performed one of Sondheim's greatest gifts to the world, a song from that show called "Move On." And interestingly, what I most want to say to Mr.

Sondheim and the artists whose work we've performed over these past ten years was best put by Sondheim himself, in that song:

>Look at all the things you've done for me:
>Opened up my eyes,
>Taught me how to see,
>Notice every tree—
>Understand the light…

Producing and directing the work of America's greatest musical theatre writers has been the most joyous, most exciting immersion training that anyone could ask for. It taught me how to direct; it taught me about life; it showed me how to write for the stage; and it made it more fun to write *about* the stage. I will always be eternally grateful, to Mr. Sondheim and his fellow artists; to the artists of New Line who have gone along on this wondrous journey for ten years; to all the people who have given us so much money to make this company operate season after season; and most of all, to the audiences of St. Louis and the surrounding region for wanting to see work like this, for supporting what we do, for coming back even if they don't love every show, for trusting us when they've never heard of a show we're producing, for being hungry for intelligent, provocative, daring, thoughtful musical theatre. New Line lives because of all of you.

We will follow Mr. Sondheim's advice. We will keep moving on. I hope you'll join us.

Scott Miller
Artistic Director
December 2001

New Line's Biggest and Most Loyal Supporters During the First Ten Years

Edward E. Adams &
 Ronald L. Pate
Ray Ammons
Robert R. Bousman &
 Ernest R. Rohay
Daniel P. Brennan
Chris Brenner &
 Tyler Olsen
David F. Butler
Dale & Judy Collier
Tracy Collins &
 Paul Schankman
Joe Collman &
 Charles Hughes
Glen, Joan, &
 Kevin Corlett
Chris & Merryl Crivelli
Thomas Defer &
 James Moll
Rick Dirkes
Pat & Tim Edmonds
Sylvia Elliott

Moritz Farbstein
Dr. Randy Ford &
 Dr. Charles Metz
John Forti & John Sweet
Mark E. Foster
Richard Frimel &
 Gary Werth
Robert Gerth
Jack Gilster
Steve Goldberg &
 J.D. Brooks
Michele Byrd Grant
Ken Haller
Slayden Harris
Rod Hartman &
 Jerry Fivian
Barbara & Jack Helmer
Alison Helmer
Bill Henke
Jerry Herman
Gordon I. Herzog
Wells & Jean Hobler

Dennis K. Hoffert &
  M. Stephen Marshall
Michael Isaacson
Christopher W. Johnson
  & Lisa K. Edwards
Steven R. Johnson
Rand Juliano
William M. Julius
Robb Kennedy
Robert Kessel
Terry Kippenberger
Karen Klaus
Rich Kluesner
Kim Kuehner
Gerry Kowarsky
Richard Lay
Barbara Liberman
Kay & Gerry Love
Susan Lukwago
Jennifer J. Luner
Michael Lunter
Ken & Judy Maxson
Jerry McAdams
Douglas McCarthy
Pat McGuire &
  Bob Sciortino
Curtis McMillen
Ken Miesner &
  John Sullivan
Howard & Penny Miller
Scott Miller
Jim Moll & Tom Defer

Robert H. Orchard
Mrs. Norman Orgel
Dr. Gustavo R.
  Valadez Ortiz
Joe & Ann Pollack
Tom & Debi Pollard
Simeon Prager, M.D.
Dr. David Prelutsky
Jeanine Prickett
Thomas W. Rich
Don J. Riehn
Ken Roberts
Dennis E. Rose
Dean, Louise, &
  Adam Rosen
John H. Russell
David Sarama &
  Vic Buzzota
Rob Semon
Quenten Schumacher &
  Steve Geiermann
L. Schwaninger &
  P. Gowdy
Deborah Sharn
Joleen Shelton
Kimi Short
Frank Siano
Stellie Siteman &
  De Kaplan
Randy Smith &
  Mike Schwartz
Stephen Sondheim

Wayne Steeves
Dr. Bill Stehnach, Jr. &
  Ray Simonl
Shelley Stewart
Mary Strauss
Justin Sweeney
Larry Terrill &
  Charlotte McKinney
Larry D. Thomas
John F. Thompson
Keith Thompson &

Dan Dowd
Nicole & Mike Trueman
James Turner
Mark Utterback
Jerry Wunderlich
Alex Young
Joseph E. Wuller
Dr. Richard D. Yoder
Larry Zerman
Sam Zinner
Heinz & Joan Zobel

Corporate Contributors

AmerenUE   American Express Financial Advisors
Anheuser-Busch Companies   Best Control Pest Control
The Composing Room   Kare for Kidz Maritz, Inc.
Midwest Digital Output   Minuteman Press
Monsanto   Music Theatre International
My Best Friend Veterinary Center   Orchard Foundation
Shaughnessy-Kniep-Hawe Paper Company
Southwestern Bell Corporation   St. Mark's Episcopal Church
Summers Printing   Heinz Zobel Associates

Celebrity Contributors

Debbie Allen   Julie Andrews   Jerry Bock
William Daniels   Fred Ebb   Michael Feinstein
Paul Gemignani   Marvin Hamlisch   Sheldon Harnick
Jerry Herman   Bob Hope   Tom Jones
Raul Julia   John Kander   James Lapine
Harold Prince   Harvey Schmidt   Stephen Sondheim
Jean Stapleton   Elaine Strich   Gwen Verdon

Board of Directors
Tracy Collins   Alison Helmer
Karen Klaus   Rick Miller
Scott Miller   Keith Price   Don J. Riehn
John H. Russell   Deborah Sharn   Keith Thompson
Honorary Members
Jerry Herman   Stephen Sondheim

About the Editor

SCOTT MILLER, the artistic director of New Line Theatre, has been directing musicals since 1981. His favorites include *Assassins, Company, Jacques Brel, March of the Falsettos, Songs for a New World, Floyd Collins, The Rocky Horror Show,* and *Hair.* He has written the book, music, and lyrics for eight musicals, and two non-musical plays. His play *Head Games* has been produced in Los Angeles, St. Louis, London, and at the Edinburgh Fringe Festival in Scotland. He has written four books on musical theatre, *From Assassins to West Side Story, Deconstructing Harold Hill, Rebels with Applause,* and *Let the Sun Shine In: The Genius of HAIR.* He has also contributed to five other theatre books, including *Stephen Sondheim: A Casebook,* a collection of essays by the leading musical theatre experts in the country. He has written one novel, *In the Blood,* based on his vampire musical of the same name. Scott also writes for national theatre magazines and arts websites, co-hosts a radio talk show about theatre, and has composed music for film, television and radio. He is a graduate of Harvard University and a member of the Dramatists Guild of America and the Society of Stage Directors and Choreographers.

0-595-26311-9